ESSENTIALS

The LOGIC *of* ENGLISH

Cursive Workbook

Pedia Learning Inc.
10800 Lyndale Ave S. Suite 181
Minneapolis, MN 55420

Cover design: Dugan Design Group
Interior design and typesetting: Katherine Lloyd, The Desk
School Font: David Occhino Design

ISBN 978-1-936706-10-5

First Edition, First Printing

10 9 8 7 6 5 4 3 2 1

www.LogicOfEnglish.com

Lesson 1

1.1 Phonogram Practice

Write the phonograms as your teacher dictates them.

1. _____   8. _____   15. _____   22. _____

2. _____   9. _____   16. _____   23. _____

3. _____   10. _____   17. _____   24. _____

4. _____   11. _____   18. _____   25. _____

5. _____   12. _____   19. _____   26. _____

6. _____   13. _____   20. _____

7. _____   14. _____   21. _____

1.2 Words Spelled with QU

Write three words that use the phonogram qu .

_____   _____   _____

1.3 Single-Letter Vowels

Write the single letter vowels.

_____   _____   _____

_____   _____   _____

LIST 1

Spelling Words	Part of Speech	Plural Past Tense
1.		
2.		
3.		
4.		
5.		
6.		
7.		
8.		
9.		
10.		
11.		
12.		
13.		
14.		
15.		

1.4 Plurals Practice

Look at the picture. Write each noun as a singular or plural.

_____

_____

_____

_____

_____

_____

_____

_____

_____

_____

_____

_____

_____

_____

_____

_____

_____

1.5 Dictation

Listen to the phrase two times. Repeat it back. Write the phrase on the lines below.

1. _____ 4. _____

2. _____ 5. _____

3. _____ 6. _____

1.6 Composition

Write six phrases using your spelling words.

1. _____

2. _____

3. _____

4. _____

5. _____

6. _____

Lesson 2

2.1 Writing the Phonograms

Write the new phonograms five times. Say them aloud as you write them.

ck

ng

ee

th

2.2 Phonogram Bingo

th	c	s	d	i
u	t	ck	r	h
k	v	e	qu	ee
w	l	n	g	p
x	y	ng	m	o

f	t	n	a	qu
s	e	b	ee	u
g	h	th	c	i
p	ck	o	j	k
ng	r	d	m	l

w	ee	g	z	ng
v	a	th	c	d
i	u	j	k	p
t	ck	o	b	e
n	s	m	r	qu

a	qu	th	f	p
r	b	u	ee	i
ng	s	g	v	w
d	c	j	k	x
ck	z	y	n	m

2.3 Phonogram Practice

Write the phonograms as your teacher dictates them.

1. _____   8. _____   15. _____

22. _____

2. _____   9. _____   16. _____

23. _____

3. _____   10. _____   17. _____

24. _____

4. _____   11. _____   18. _____

25. _____

5. _____   12. _____   19. _____

6. _____   13. _____   20. _____

7. _____   14. _____   21. _____

2.4 Vowels

Write the single-letter vowels.

_____   _____   _____

_____   _____   _____

2.5 Short Vowels

Write the short vowels.

_____   _____   _____

_____   _____

2.6 Long Vowels

Write the long vowels.

_____   _____   _____

_____   _____

2.7 Words That Use CK

Read the words aloud.

deck	rock	tack
neck	sock	rack
lick	truck	
tick	luck	

2.8 Words That Do Not Use CK

Read the words aloud.

cheek	Greek	seek
creek	week	sleek

LIST 2

	Spelling Words	Part of Speech	Plural Past Tense
1.			
2.			
3.			
4.			
5.			
6.			
7.			
8.			
9.			
10.			
11.			
12.			
13.			
14.			
15.			

2.9 Plurals Practice

Look at the picture. Write the plural.

_____

_____

_____

_____

_____

_____

2.10 Identifying Nouns and Adjectives

Label the parts of speech in your workbook as your teacher writes them on the board.

1. big tree   *2.* three rocks   *3.* long path

2.11 Dictation

Listen to each phrase as your teacher dictates. Repeat it back. Write it on the lines below.

1. _____

2. _____

3. _____

4. _____

5. _____

6. _____

2.12 Composition

Write six adjective, noun phrases using your spelling words.

1. _____

2. _____

3. _____

4. _____

5. _____

6. _____

2.13 Compound Words

Write the compound word formed by the two words.

1. *black + top = blacktop*
2. *back + street =*
3. *hand + bag =*
4. *hand + spring =*
5. *hot + dog =*
6. *flat + bed =*
7. *sun + set =*
8. *cat + nap =*
9. *dog + sled =*
10. *sand + box =*

Lesson 3

3.1 Writing the Phonograms

Write the new phonograms five times. Say them aloud as you write them.

er _____

or _____

ea _____

sh _____

3.2 Phonogram Practice

Write the phonograms as your teacher dictates them.

1. _____   6. _____   11. _____   16. _____

2. _____   7. _____   12. _____   17. _____

3. _____   8. _____   13. _____   18. _____

4. _____   9. _____   14. _____   19. _____

5. _____   10. _____   15. _____   20. _____

3.3 Long Vowel Sounds

Write the long vowel sounds as your teacher dictates them.

1. _____   3. _____   5. _____

2. _____   4. _____

3.4 Short Vowel Sounds

Write the short vowel sounds as your teacher dictates them.

1. _____   3. _____   5. _____

2. _____   4. _____

LIST 3

	Spelling Words	Part of Speech	Plural Past Tense
1.			
2.			
3.			
4.			
5.			
6.			
7.			
8.			
9.			
10.			
11.			
12.			
13.			
14.			
15.			

3.5 Dictation

Listen to each phrase as your teacher dictates. Repeat it back. Write it on the lines below.

1. _____

2. _____

3. _____

4. _____

5. _____

6. _____

3.6 Composition

Write six adjective, noun phrases using your spelling words.

1. _____

2. _____

3. _____

4. _____

5. _____

6. _____

3.7 O'clock Times

Write each of the times in words.

3:00 _____

6:00 _____

10:00 _____

7:00 _____

3.8 Compound Words

Write the compound word formed by the two words.

1. sand + paper = sandpaper _____

2. butter + milk = _____

3. milk + man = _____

4. bread + stick = _____

5. paper + back = _____

6. corn + bread = _____

7. clean + up = _____

8. hand + bag = _____

9. hand + spring = _____

10. bread + basket = _____

Lesson 4

4.1 Writing the Phonograms

Write the new phonograms five times each and say them aloud.

ai _____

ay _____

oy _____

oi _____

4.2 Phonogram Practice

Write the phonograms as your teacher dictates them.

1. _____	7. _____	13. _____	19. _____
2. _____	8. _____	14. _____	20. _____
3. _____	9. _____	15. _____	
4. _____	10. _____	16. _____	
5. _____	11. _____	17. _____	
6. _____	12. _____	18. _____	

4.3 Phonogram Board Game

Play the game using your teacher's directions.

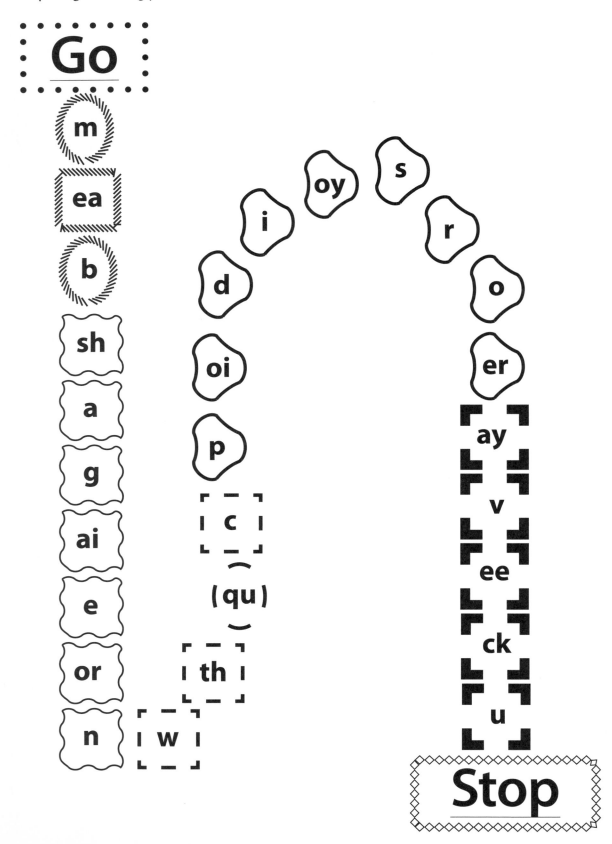

4.4 Consonants and Vowels

Write the multi-letter consonants and vowels in the correct column.

th, ck, ee, ea, sh, ai, ng, ay, oi, oy

Consonants	Vowels
_____	_____
_____	_____
_____	_____
_____	_____
	_____
	_____

4.5 A Says /ă/

Read the words. Mark the vowel sound that A spells at the end of the syllable.

ma	pa	sofa	spa
orca	data	lava	toga

4.6 Spellings of the Long /ā/ sound

Write the spellings of the long /ā/ sound.

_____   _____   _____   _____

Where is each spelling most commonly used?

End of the Syllable	Middle of the Syllable	End of the Word

LIST 4

	Spelling Words	Part of Speech	Plural Past Tense
1.			
2.			
3.			
4.			
5.			
6.			
7.			
8.			
9.			
10.			
11.			
12.			
13.			
14.			
15.			

4.7 Article Adjectives

Write the article adjectives.

_____   _____   _____

4.8 Identifying Nouns and Adjectives

the gray paint

a long train

the plain oil

4.9 Vocabulary Development

Add the ending $\boxed{\text{-er}}$ and $\boxed{\text{-est}}$ to each word.

quick	strong	black	plain
clean	green	pink	gray

quicker

quickest

4.10 Dictation

Listen to each phrase as your teacher dictates. Repeat it back. Write it on the lines below.

1. _____

2. _____

3. _____

4. _____

5. _____

6. _____

4.11 Composition

Write six article, adjective, noun phrases using your spelling words.

the plainest camp _____

1. _____

2. _____

3. _____

4. _____

5. _____

6. _____

Lesson 5

5.1 Assessment

Listen to each phrase as your teacher dictates. Repeat it back. Write it on the lines below.

1. _____

2. _____

3. _____

4. _____

5. _____

6. _____

7. _____

8. _____

9. _____

10. _____

11. _____

12. _____

13. _____

14. _____

15. _____

5.2 Reading

Read the words and phrases.

1. bat
2. hat
3. list
4. frozen milk
5. soft bed
6. a pink quilt
7. a hero

8. ten strings
9. mailman
10. street
11. dog
12. forest
13. plain oil
14. clock

15. favor
16. human hands
17. bread
18. ponds
19. rainforest
20. the hot sun

5.3 Words to practice

Mark the spelling words which need more practice.

1. _____ a	21. _____ green	41. _____ quick
2. _____ an	22. _____ hand	42. _____ quilt
3. _____ bad	23. _____ hat	43. _____ rain
4. _____ bag	24. _____ hero	44. _____ rock
5. _____ bat	25. _____ human	45. _____ seven
6. _____ bed	26. _____ last	46. _____ ship
7. _____ black	27. _____ leg	47. _____ sick
8. _____ boy	28. _____ list	48. _____ six
9. _____ bread	29. _____ long	49. _____ soft
10. _____ cat	30. _____ mail	50. _____ street
11. _____ clean	31. _____ man	51. _____ string
12. _____ clock	32. _____ map	52. _____ strong
13. _____ day	33. _____ milk	53. _____ sun
14. _____ dog	34. _____ oil	54. _____ ten
15. _____ duck	35. _____ paint	55. _____ the
16. _____ fast	36. _____ paper	56. _____ three
17. _____ favor	37. _____ path	57. _____ toy
18. _____ forest	38. _____ pink	58. _____ train
19. _____ frozen	39. _____ plain	59. _____ tree
20. _____ gray	40. _____ pond	60. _____ truck

5.4 Vowels at the End of Syllables

Read each word. Draw a line to divide the syllables. Mark the long and short vowel sounds.

1.	pepper	*8.*	popper
2.	paper	*9.*	supper
3.	after	*10.*	coffin
4.	favor	*11.*	caper
5.	offer	*12.*	topaz
6.	open	*13.*	frozen
7.	happen	*14.*	human

5.5 Plurals

As your teacher dictates the words, write the singular form in the first column and the plural form in the second column.

Singular	Plurals
1.	
2.	
3.	
4.	
5.	
6.	
7.	
8.	
9.	
10.	
11.	
12.	
13.	
14.	
15.	

5.6 Phonogram Quiz

Write the phonograms as your teacher dictates them.

1. _____	11. _____	21. _____	31. _____
2. _____	12. _____	22. _____	32. _____
3. _____	13. _____	23. _____	33. _____
4. _____	14. _____	24. _____	34. _____
5. _____	15. _____	25. _____	35. _____
6. _____	16. _____	26. _____	36. _____
7. _____	17. _____	27. _____	37. _____
8. _____	18. _____	28. _____	38. _____
9. _____	19. _____	29. _____	
10. _____	20. _____	30. _____	

5.7 Phonogram Blitz

Lesson 6

6

6.1 Writing the Phonograms

Write the new phonograms five times each and say them aloud.

ar _____

ch _____

oo _____

6.2 Phonogram Practice

Write the phonograms as your teacher dictates them.

1. _____   6. _____   11. _____   16. _____

2. _____   7. _____   12. _____   17. _____

3. _____   8. _____   13. _____   18. _____

4. _____   9. _____   14. _____   19. _____

5. _____   10. _____   15. _____   20. _____

6.3 Reading the Vowel Sounds

Read the vowel sounds aloud.

ŭ	ü	ă	ā
ŏ	ä	ē	
ĕ	ö	ū	

6.4 Writing the Vowel Sounds

Write the vowel sounds as your teacher dictates them.

1. _____   *4.* _____   *7.* _____   *10.* _____

2. _____   *5.* _____   *8.* _____

3. _____   *6.* _____   *9.* _____

6.5 Discover the Rule

Read the words. Look for a pattern. Circle the four words that do not use a short vowel sound.

staff	tall	class
sniff	call	mess
scoff	pill	miss
off	ball	moss
huff	fall	glass
puff	pull	pass
scruff	hill	bass

6.6 Consonants and Vowels

Write the multi-letter consonants and vowels in the correct column.

th, ck, ng, ee, ea, sh, ai, ay, oi, oy, ch, oo

Consonants	Vowels

LIST 6

Spelling Words	Part of Speech	Plural Past Tense
1.		
2.		
3.		
4.		
5.		
6.		
7.		
8.		
9.		
10.		
11.		
12.		
13.		
14.		
15.		

6.7 Plurals

Look at the picture. Write the plural.

_____

_____

_____

_____

_____

_____

6.8 Identifying Parts of Speech

Read the phrases. Label the parts of speech while your teacher writes them on the board.

a full moon

the secret classroom

a glass ball

6.9 Commas in a Series

Read the lists. Circle the commas.

1. sun and moon

2. cars and trucks

3. balls, cards, toys, and books

4. paper, paint, and paintbrushes

5. seven men, three boys, and ten kids

6. black trucks, red cars, and gray trains

6.10 Commas in a Series

Add commas where needed to each of the lists.

1. rivers hills and cliffs

2. paper and cards

3. trains trucks cars and boats

4. milk bread and butter

5. ten ducks seven dogs and three fish

6.11 Dictation

Listen to each phrase as your teacher dictates. Repeat it back. Write it on the lines below.

1. _____

   _____

2. _____

   _____

3. _____

   _____

4. _____

   _____

5. _____

   _____

6. _____

   _____

6.12 Vocabulary Development

_____

6.13 Compound Words

Form 10 new compound words.

cannon	basket	hair	mark
meat	school	brush	shelf
boy	flash	glasses	room
tooth	book	ball	
sun	text	card	
class	paint	end	

1. _____

2. _____

3. _____

4. _____

5. _____

6. _____

7. _____

8. _____

9. _____

10. _____

6.14 Composition

Choose three or more words. Combine them into a list.

toothbrush	milk	hands
glasses	dogs	cliffs
soap	camps	streets
balls	oil	feet
schools	legs	ducks
parks	bread	rivers
books	paths	balloons
classes	hills	

toothbrush, soap, and glasses

1. _____

2. _____

3. _____

4. _____

5. _____

6. _____

Lesson 7

7.1 Writing the Phonograms

Write the new phonograms five times each and say them aloud.

oa _____

oe _____

7.2 Phonogram Practice

Write the phonograms as your teacher dictates them.

1. _____   6. _____   11. _____   16. _____

2. _____   7. _____   12. _____   17. _____

3. _____   8. _____   13. _____   18. _____

4. _____   9. _____   14. _____   19. _____

5. _____   10. _____   15. _____   20. _____

7.3 Spellings of the Long /ō/ Sound

_____   _____   _____

Most Common Spellings of O

Middle of the syllable	End of the syllable
_____	_____

Important words to remember OE

_____   _____

_____   _____

_____   _____

_____

Important words to remember OO

_____   _____

7.4 Plurals Practice

Read the word in the first column. Write the plural form in the second column.

Singular	Plurals
1. *flash*	
2. *hat*	
3. *boy*	
4. *train*	
5. *class*	
6. *card*	
7. *book*	
8. *loss*	
9. *school*	
10. *perch*	
11. *buzz*	
12. *beach*	
13. *secret*	
14. *glass*	
15. *park*	

7.5 Extra Practice: Double F, L and S

Write as many words as you can think of which end in _ill, _all, and _ull.

_ill	_all
_____	_____
_____	_____
_____	_____
_____	_____
_____	_____
_____	_____
_____	_____
_____	**_ull**
_____	_____
_____	_____
_____	_____
_____	_____
_____	_____

LIST 7

Spelling Words	Part of Speech	Plural Past Tense
1.		
2.		
3.		
4.		
5.		
6.		
7.		
8.		
9.		
10.		
11.		
12.		
13.		
14.		
15.		

7.6 Articles

Read the phrases aloud. Circle the consonant that follows "a" with red and circle the vowel that follows "an" with blue in each of the phrases.

a river	an ant
a hill	an egg
a road	an inch
a cheap coat	an open door
a clean room	an oil lamp

7.7 A and An

Complete the phrase using "a" or "an."

1. _____ open room

2. _____ basketball

3. _____ egg

4. _____ inch long nail

5. _____ tall door

6. _____ cheap coat

7.8 Identifying Parts of Speech

Read the phrases. Write the parts of speech while your teacher writes them on the board.

a boat, a car, and a truck

a long road and a short hill

a red, black, and green coat

7.9 Dictation

Listen to each phrase as your teacher dictates. Repeat it back. Write it on the lines below.

1. _____

_____

2. _____

_____

3. _____

_____

4. _____

_____

5. _____

_____

6. _____

_____

7.10 Compound Words

Combine the words in each box to form new compound words.

	bell
	mat
door	step
	way

1. _____

2. _____

3. _____

4. _____

sail	
tug	
motor	boat
river	

1. _____

2. _____

3. _____

4. _____

bed	
class	room
bath	
play	

1. _____

2. _____

3. _____

4. _____

Extra Practice

7.11 The Suffixes -er and -est

Add the ending -er and -est to each word.

~~quick~~	tall	rich	sharp
cheap	full	poor	gray

1. *quicker*   *quickest*

2. _____   _____

3. _____   _____

4. _____   _____

5. _____   _____

6. _____   _____

7. _____   _____

8. _____   _____

7.12 Composition

Write six phrases using the words below for ideas.

a	cheap	egg
an	tall	rock
the	open	boat
	glass	coat
	secret	road
	full	room
	poor	door
	black	floor

1. _____

2. _____

3. _____

4. _____

5. _____

6. _____

Lesson 8

8.1 The Phonogram WH

Read each word. Underline the WH. Where is it used in the word?

when	whip	wheel	whisk
wheat	whiff	which	whimper

8.2 The Phonogram W

Read each word below. Compare the sound made by the phonogram W to the sound made by the phonogram WH.

water	week	wool	wall
warm	wing	wind	wax

8.3 Writing the Phonograms

Write the new phonograms five times each and say them aloud.

igh

wh

8.4 Phonogram Practice

While your teacher dictates the phonograms, write them on the bingo card below.

8.5 Phonograms Ending in GH

Read the words. Underline IGH. Where is it used?

blight	high	plight	tight
bright	light	right	thigh
fight	might	sigh	
flight	nigh	sight	
fright	night	slight	

Extra Practice

8.6 Write the IGH Words

Write the seventeen IGH words. Use the following phonograms to give you a hint. Cross out each one as you use it.

b	l	s	t
b	l	s	t
f	m	s	t
f	n	t	t
f	n	t	t
h	p	t	t
l	r	t	t
l	r	t	t
l	r	t	th

1. _____

2. _____

3. _____

4. _____

5. _____

6. _____

7. _____

8. _____

9. _____

10. _____

11. _____

12. _____

13. _____

14. _____

15. _____

16. _____

17. _____

LIST 8

Spelling Words	Part of Speech	Plural Past Tense
1.		
2.		
3.		
4.		
5.		
6.		
7.		
8.		
9.		
10.		
11.		
12.		
13.		
14.		
15.		

8.7 Identifying Parts of Speech

Read the phrases. Mark the parts of speech with your teacher.

the best wheat

good wheels, bright lights, and the best music

a perfect day and a perfect night

8.8 Comparison

Read the phrases. Discuss them with your teacher. Put an A over the article adjective. Underline the suffix.

a warm coat

a warmer coat

the warmest coat

a clean room

a cleaner room

the cleanest room

8.9 Editing

Find the mistake in each phrase. Rewrite the phrase correctly on the lines below.

1. a gooder program

_____

2. the dogs cats, and fish

_____

3. a red, black and green coat

_____

4. the goodest night

_____

5. a brightest light

_____

6. the trains, boats and cars

_____

7. a tallest cliffs

_____

8. the bestest music

_____

8.10 Dictation

Listen to each phrase as your teacher dictates. Repeat it back. Write it on the lines below.

1. _____

_____

2. _____

_____

3. _____

_____

4. _____

_____

5. _____

_____

6. _____

_____

8.11 Composition

Choose a word from each column. Compose three phrases.

the	good	program
a	best	music
	better	night
	perfect	wheel
		block

the perfect program

1. _____

2. _____

3. _____

Choose a word or suffix from each column. Compose three phrases.

the	bright	-er	cliff
a	light	-est	moon
	tall		soap
	cheap		coat
	warm		night

a lighter coat

1. _____

2. _____

3. _____

8.12 Vocabulary Development

Add the endings -ish and -ness to each word.

1. sick + ish = sickish
2. black + ish = blackish
3. gray + ish = grayish
4. boy + ish = boyish
5. sick + ness = sickness
6. boyish + ness = boyishness
7. quick + ness = quickness
8. clean + ness = cleaness cleaness
9. sharp + ness = sharpness
10. bright + ness = brightness

Lesson 9

9.1 AUGH Words

Read each word. Underline the AUGH.

caught   slaughter   fraught

daughter   taught

Read each word. Underline the AUGH.

laugh   laughter

9.2 AU Words

Read the words with AU. Draw a line between the syllables. Underline the AU. Where is it commonly used within the word?

author	caulk	haunt
aunt	fault	taunt
auto	maul	launch
automatic	vault	summersault
haul	restaurant	

9.3 AW Words

Read the words with AW. Underline the AW. Where is it commonly used within the word?

claw	crawl	dawn	awful
jaw	shawl	fawn	awkward
flaw	awl	drawn	awning
raw	brawl	pawn	hawk
law	drawl	sawn	squawk
saw		yawn	gawk
straw		lawn	
draw			

9.4 Writing the Phonograms

Write the new phonograms five times each and say them aloud.

au _____

aw _____

augh _____

9.5 Phonogram Practice

Write the phonograms as your teacher dictates them.

1. _____   6. _____   11. _____   16. _____

2. _____   7. _____   12. _____   17. _____

3. _____   8. _____   13. _____   18. _____

4. _____   9. _____   14. _____   19. _____

5. _____   10. _____   15. _____   20. _____

9.6 Phonogram Tic-Tac-Toe

au	augh	aw
sh	igh	er
wh	oy	ea

ar	oo	aw
sh	au	or
oy	ch	augh

ar	oe	oy
wh	oo	oa
augh	oi	or

wh	sh	ar
augh	ai	aw
oy	oi	ay

au	ai	oi
aw	ay	oy
igh	oe	oa

oe	augh	au
or	igh	ch
er	sh	ea

9.7 A says /ä/

Read the words in your workbook and put two dots over the /ä/.

water   wash   ball   fall

wasp   walnut   call

wall

9.8 Spellings of the /ä/ Sound

What are the five ways to spell the /ä/ sound?

1. _____   3. _____   5. _____

2. _____   4. _____

9.9 Most Common Spellings of /ä/

End of the Syllable	Middle of the syllable	End of the Word
_____	_____	_____

LIST 9

Spelling Words	Part of Speech	Plural Past Tense
1.		
2.		
3.		
4.		
5.		
6.		
7.		
8.		
9.		
10.		
11.		
12.		
13.		
14.		
15.		

9.10 Identifying Parts of Speech

Read the phrases. Mark the parts of speech with your teacher.

the author's greatest book

the room's darkest corner

mother's laughter

9.11 Possessive Practice

Read each phrase. Write the apostrophe in the correct place.

1.   the teachers classroom

2.   the mans coat

3.   the mens coats

4.   three boys toys

5.   ten sailors boats

6.   mothers brown dress

7.   grandfathers yard

8.   the schools ball

9.12 Article Review

Combine the articles "a" and "an" with the nouns below to form eight phrases.

a

an

mother

father

author

sister

aunt

egg

inch

program

law

a mother

1. _____

2. _____

3. _____

4. _____

5. _____

6. _____

7. _____

8. _____

9.13 Editing

Find the mistake in each phrase. Rewrite the phrase correctly on the lines below.

1. mothers laughter

_____

2. the graitest year

_____

3. the authors greatest book

_____

4. days, and nights

_____

5. the rit law

_____

6. greatgreatgrandmother

_____

7. mothers fathers, sons, and daughters

_____

_____

9.14 Composition

Write six phrases which show possession using the words below.

the	father	glasses
a	mother	room
an	author	light
	sister	music
	aunt	program
	son	book
	daughter	train
	school	yard
		son

the father's glasses

1. _____

2. _____

3. _____

4. _____

5. _____

6. _____

9.15 Vocabulary Development

Complete the pairs of family members.

brother and

sister

mother and

_____

grandfather and

_____

great-grandmother and

_____

stepmother and

_____

stepbrother and

_____

great-great-grandfather and

_____

stepdaughter and

_____

daughter and

_____

grandson and

_____

9.16 *Son* **and** *Sun*

Draw a picture and label with each of these words.

9.17 Dictation

Listen to each phrase as your teacher dictates. Repeat it back. Write it on the lines below.

1. _____

_____

2. _____

_____

3. _____

_____

4. _____

_____

5. _____

_____

6. _____

_____

Lesson 10

10

10.1 Assessment

Listen to each phrase as your teacher dictates. Repeat it back. Write it on the lines below.

1. _____

2. _____

3. _____

4. _____

5. _____

6. _____

7. _____

8. _____

9. _____

10. _____

11. _____

12. _____

13. _____

14. _____

15. _____

10.2 Reading

Read the words and phrases.

1. cheaper cards

2. seven warm coats

3. the music program

4. raw eggs

5. clean floors

6. the pink door

7. the black truck's wheels

8. good laws

9. bright moonlight

10. six years, three weeks, and ten days

11. grandmothers, mothers, sisters, and aunts

12. ten toes

13. brother's toy blocks

14. tall men

15. poor

16. wheat, soap, and eggs

17. ball

18. six inches

10.3 Words to practice

Mark the spelling words which need more practice.

1. ___ all	23. ___ father	45. ___ road
2. ___ aunt	24. ___ floor	46. ___ room
3. ___ author	25. ___ full	47. ___ school
4. ___ ball	26. ___ glass	48. ___ secret
5. ___ best	27. ___ good	49. ___ sharp
6. ___ better	28. ___ great	50. ___ sister
7. ___ block	29. ___ hill	51. ___ soap
8. ___ boat	30. ___ inch	52. ___ son
9. ___ book	31. ___ laughter	53. ___ tall
10. ___ bright	32. ___ law	54. ___ toe
11. ___ brother	33. ___ light	55. ___ tooth
12. ___ brush	34. ___ moon	56. ___ warm
13. ___ car	35. ___ mother	57. ___ wheat
14. ___ card	36. ___ music	58. ___ wheel
15. ___ cheap	37. ___ night	59. ___ yard
16. ___ class	38. ___ perfect	60. ___ year
17. ___ cliff	39. ___ poor	
18. ___ coat	40. ___ program	
19. ___ corner	41. ___ raw	
20. ___ daughter	42. ___ rich	
21. ___ door	43. ___ right	
22. ___ egg	44. ___ river	

10.4 Word Search

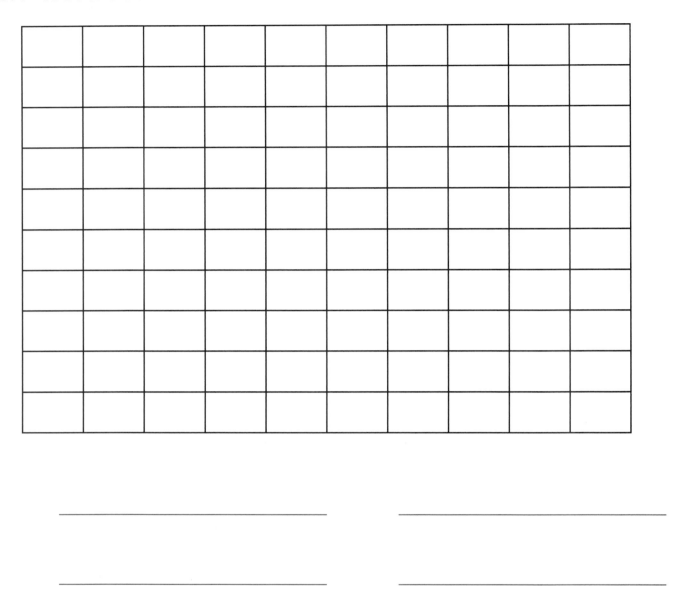

10.5 Plurals Review

Write the plural form of each word.

Spelling Words	Plurals
1. author	
2. brush	
3. forest	
4. school	
5. secret	
6. glass	
7. inch	
8. classroom	
9. sister	
10. egg	

10.6 Possessives

Combine the words to form eight new possessive phrases.

a	brother	school
an	boy	class
the	sister	glasses
six	man	music
ten	dog	room
three	aunt	toy
seven	book	hat

six boys' toys

1. _____

2. _____

3. _____

4. _____

5. _____

6. _____

7. _____

8. _____

Extra Practice

10.7 More Possessives

To indicate if the possessive is singular or plural. Write an S if is singular and a P if it is plural.

1. the mother's coat   _____

2. Fathers' Day   _____

3. Grandmother's yard _____

4. the school's ball   _____

5. the boys' trains   _____

6. the sisters' bedroom _____

10.8 Phonogram Quiz

Write the phonograms as your teacher dictates them.

1. _____	13. _____	25. _____	37. _____
2. _____	14. _____	26. _____	38. _____
3. _____	15. _____	27. _____	39. _____
4. _____	16. _____	28. _____	40. _____
5. _____	17. _____	29. _____	41. _____
6. _____	18. _____	30. _____	42. _____
7. _____	19. _____	31. _____	43. _____
8. _____	20. _____	32. _____	44. _____
9. _____	21. _____	33. _____	45. _____
10. _____	22. _____	34. _____	46. _____
11. _____	23. _____	35. _____	47. _____
12. _____	24. _____	36. _____	48. _____

10.9 Speed Bingo

Lesson 11

11.1 Writing the Phonograms

Write the new phonograms five times each and say them aloud.

ou _____

ow _____

ough _____

_____

11.2 Phonogram Practice

Write the phonograms as your teacher dictates them.

1. _____   6. _____   11. _____   16. _____

2. _____   7. _____   12. _____   17. _____

3. _____   8. _____   13. _____   18. _____

4. _____   9. _____   14. _____   19. _____

5. _____   10. _____   15. _____   20. _____

11.3 Phonogram Board Game

Play the phonogram game using the directions provided by your teacher.

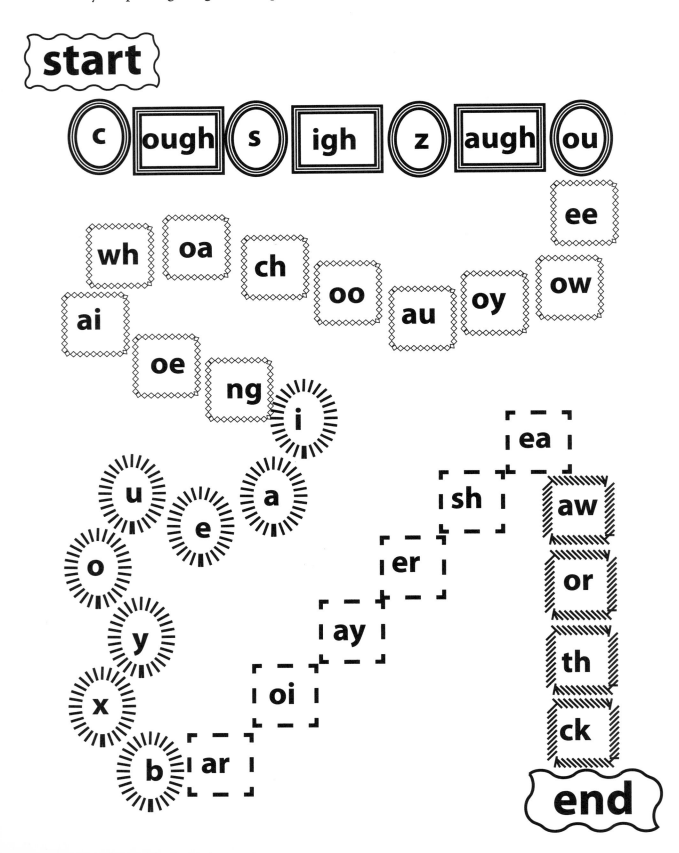

11.4 Reading Words with OW

Read the words aloud. Underline the OW.

/ow/		/ō/	
cow	town	throw	window
brown	crown	thrown	show
down	powder	grow	snow
frown	tower	grown	crow

11.5 Reading Words with OU

Read the words aloud. Underline the OU.

/ow/	/ō/	/oo/	/ŭ/
out	your	tour	young
count	soul	group	touch
cloud			
shout			
found			
ground			
noun			

11.6 Reading Words with OUGH

Read the words aloud. Underline the OUGH.

/ŏ/	/ō/	/oo/	/ow/
bought	although	through	bough
thought	dough		drought
fought	borough		
ought	furlough	**/ŭff/**	**/ŏff/**
nought	thorough	enough	cough
wrough		rough	trough

11.7 Most Common Spellings of /ow/

Write the spellings for the sound /ow/.

Middle of the Syllable	End of the Word
_____	_____

LIST 11

Spelling Words	Part of Speech	Plural Past Tense
1.		
2.		
3.		
4.		
5.		
6.		
7.		
8.		
9.		
10.		
11.		
12.		
13.		
14.		
15.		

11.8 Identifying Parts of Speech

Mark the parts of speech.

The daughters sing.

The boys play.

a long train

sing, shout , play

11.9 Sentences and Fragments

Rewrite the sentences with a capital letter and end mark. Do not do anything if it is a fragment.

1. the sisters whisper

   _____

2. three sick brothers

   _____

3. mother agrees

   _____

4. six boys march

   _____

5. the long path

   _____

11.10 Sentences and Fragments

Write an S next to the complete sentences. Write F next to the fragments.

1. _____ The boys play.

2. _____ Sister-in-laws.

3. _____ The men agree.

4. _____ Mother coughs.

5. _____ The cleanest bedroom.

6. _____ The trucks destroy.

7. _____ Whisper and shout.

8. _____ The hero helps the small boys.

9. _____ The door opens.

10. _____ Mother and Father wait.

11.11 Reading Practice

Read each sentence. Circle the capital letter and period.

The boys play.

Grandmother and Grandfather agree.

The cats hide.

The brothers and sisters skate.

Mother and Father help.

The men sing.

11.12 Subject-Verb Agreement

Write the correct ending for the verb if needed.

1. A dog sleep_____.

2. The goats eat _____.

3. The boys jump_____.

4. The bee buzz_____.

5. The dog growl_____.

6. The mothers whisper_____.

7. The band march_____.

8. The fathers sing _____.

9. An aunt smile_____.

10. The boy walk _____.

11.13 Dictation

Listen to each sentence as your teacher reads it aloud. Repeat it back. Write it on the lines below.

1. _____

2. _____

3. _____

4. _____

5. _____

6. _____

11.14 Composition

Write six sentences with a subject, verb, capital letter and end mark. Use words from Spelling Lists 9 and 11.

1. _____

2. _____

3. _____

4. _____

5. _____

6. _____

11.15 Writing with Adjectives

Underline the subject. Think of an adjective that describes it. Rewrite the sentence.

1.   The <u>cat</u> sits.

   The gray cat sits.

2.   A duck quacks.

   _____

3.   The river flows.

   _____

4.   The class laughs.

   _____

5.   The clock ticks.

   _____

11.16 Vocabulary Development

Write the new word formed by adding the suffix -less or -full.

1. _paper + less =_ _____
2. _son + less =_ _____
3. _help + less =_ helples _____
4. _mother + less =_ _____
5. _help + ful =_ _____
6. _play + ful =_ _____
7. _bag + ful =_ _____
8. _glass + ful =_ _____

Lesson 12

12.1 Writing the Phonograms

Write the new phonogram five times and say it aloud.

tch

12.2 Phonogram Practice

Write the phonograms as your teacher dictates them.

1. tch   6. _____   11. _____   16. _____

2. tch   7. _____   12. _____   17. _____

3. tch   8. _____   13. _____   18. _____

4. tch   9. _____   14. _____   19. _____

5. _____   10. _____   15. _____   20. _____

12.3 Words Ending in -ALK

Read the words. Underline the silent L twice and mark the A with the correct vowel sound.

talk	chalk	balk
walk	stalk	

12.4 TCH Words

Read the words. Underline the TCH. Mark the vowels.

catch	itch	sketch	switch
fetch	match	scratch	watch
hutch	patch	stitch	butcher

LIST 12

Spelling Words	Part of Speech	Plural Past Tense
1.		
2.		
3.		
4.		
5.		
6.		
7.		
8.		
9.		
10.		
11.		
12.		
13.		
14.		
15.		

12.5 Identifying Parts of Speech

Label the parts of speech with your teacher.

The man pushes the swing.

The sisters enjoy the book.

Mother opens the green box.

The three boys eat bread and jam.

Extra Practice

12.6 Reading Sentences

Read the sentences aloud.

1. The boys eat good food.

2. Sister pushes the swing.

3. Mother calls Grandfather.

4. The dog destroys the chair.

5. The small ducks follow the mother duck.

6. The man throws the ball.

7. Brother opens the door.

Extra Practice

12.7 Subject-Verb Agreement

Write the correct ending for the verb if needed.

1. The author enjoy_____ books.

2. Mother read _____ the paper.

3. The boys throw_____ the ball.

4. The cats follow_____ the dog.

5. The door open_____.

6. The men eat _____ the bread.

7. The teachers watch_____ the class.

8. Father want_____ the car.

9. Grandpa throw _____ the ball.

10. Mother enjoy_____ the program.

12.8 Sentences and Fragments

Write an S next to the complete sentences. Write F next to the fragments.

1. _____   The dog sleeps.

2. _____   Great grandmother.

3. _____   The dog follows the ducks.

4. _____   Quick boys run.

5. _____   The cleanest truck.

6. _____   The man eats lunch.

7. _____   Play, sing, shout.

8. _____   Father teaches the dog tricks.

9. _____   The open door.

10. _____   The children throw the ball.

12.9 Vocabulary Development

Add -er to each of the words.

play	follow	open	fight
catch	wait	sing	call

1. _____

2. _____

3. _____

4. _____

5. _____

6. _____

7. _____

8. _____

12.10 Dictation

Listen to each sentence as your teacher reads it aloud. Repeat it back. Write it on the lines below.

1. _____

_____

2. _____

_____

3. _____

_____

4. _____

_____

5. _____

_____

6. _____

_____

12.11 Composition

Write six sentences which include a subject, verb and direct object. Use the words below.

class	push	popcorn
boy	enjoy	book
man	eat	program
grandfather	open	swing
duck	call	ball
grandmother	read	boy
teacher	catch	paper

Grandfather calls the boy.

1. _____

2. _____

3. _____

4. _____

5. _____

6. _____

12.12 Writing with Adjectives

Underline the subject and the direct object. Think of an adjective that describes each one and re-write the sentence.

1. The <u>teacher</u> reads a <u>book</u>.

    The math teacher reads a thick book.

2. The catcher throws the ball.

3. The helpers enjoy the program.

4. A player swings the bat.

5. The class plays music.

Lesson 13

13

13.1 Words with KN and GN

Read the words. Underline the KN and GN.

kn	gn
knead	gnat
knack	gnaw
knight	gnarl
know	gnash
knock	gnome
knob	campaign
knot	sign
knit	design
knee	

13.2 Writing the Phonograms

Write the new phonograms five times each and say them aloud.

kn _____

gn _____

13.3 Phonogram Practice

Write the phonograms as your teacher dictates them.

1. _____	6. _____	11. _____	16. _____
2. _____	7. _____	12. _____	17. _____
3. _____	8. _____	13. _____	18. _____
4. _____	9. _____	14. _____	19. _____
5. _____	10. _____	15. _____	20. _____

13.4 I and O

Read the words. Mark the I and O with their long vowel sound.

/ī/	/ō/
wild	bold
child	cold
mild	gold
blind	roll
kind	both
sign	bolt

13.5 I and O Continued

Read the words. Mark the I and O with their short vowel sound.

/ĭ/	/ŏ/
bill	lock
milk	golf
sick	doll
drink	sock

13.6 Rhyming

Write words that rhyme on the lines below.

song   *cold*

_____   _____

_____   _____

_____   _____

_____   _____

sink   *blind*

_____   _____

_____   _____

_____   _____

_____   _____

LIST 13

	Spelling Words	Part of Speech	Plural Past Tense
1.			
2.			
3.			
4.			
5.			
6.			
7.			
8.			
9.			
10.			
11.			
12.			
13.			
14.			
15.			

13.7 Sentences and Fragments

Write an S next to the complete sentences. Write an F next to the fragments.

1. _____ The boy designs a boat.

2. _____ The tall boy.

3. _____ Great sons and daughters.

4. _____ Mother knows the music.

5. _____ Father finds the bread.

6. _____ The man holds the door.

7. _____ Cats, dogs, frogs, and lizards.

8. _____ Grandpa drinks the milk.

9. _____ Students know the book.

10. _____ Sees the boat.

13.8 Identifying Parts of Speech

Answer the questions your teacher asks and mark the parts of speech.

The grandmother knows the boy.

The boy knows the grandmother.

The brothers sell good books.

The six men sell cheap cars and trucks.

13.9 Subject-Verb Agreement

Write the correct ending for the verb if needed.

1.   The men search_____.

2.   A child jump _____.

3.   A girl turn_____.

4.   The flowers need_____ .

5.   The coat match_____ the shoes.

6.   The birds eat _____ the seeds.

7.   The children sing _____ a song.

8.   The designer draw _____.

9.   The man open_____ the door.

10. The girl catch _____ the ball.

13.10 Editing

Find the errors. Rewrite each sentence correctly.

1.   Father Mother Grandfather and Grandmother sign the papers.

_____

_____

2.   the cats drink milk

_____

_____

3.   The teacher needs pens paper markers and paint.

_____

_____

4.   the child draws cats dogs and ducks.

_____

_____

5.   The students draw cats ducks and dogs.

_____

_____

6.   The children run shout jump and play

_____

_____

13.11 Dictation

Listen to each sentence as your teacher reads it aloud. Repeat it back. Write it on the lines below.

1. _____

_____

2. _____

_____

3. _____

_____

4. _____

_____

5. _____

_____

6. _____

_____

13.12 Composition

Write 6 sentences with a subject, verb, direct object.

father	find	bread
mother	pull	boat
author	sell	book
dog	design	song
truck	pick	music
boy	need	toy
helper	sing	cat
duck	follow	string

Father sells books.

1. _____

2. _____

3. _____

4. _____

5. _____

6. _____

13.13 Vocabulary

Write six new words by adding the prefix re- to the following words.

	call
	open
re-	play
	start
	sell
	draw

1. _____

2. _____

3. _____

4. _____

5. _____

6. _____

Lesson 14

14.1 Spellings of /er/

Read the words. Underline the phonogram that spells the sound /er/.

ir	ur	ear
first	fur	earth
bird	burn	learn
skirt	hurt	pearl
stir	turn	earn
shirt	church	yearn
squirrel	burst	search
birth	curl	heard

14.2 R or a Spelling of /er/?

Read the words. As you read them, compare the vowel sounds.

print	perch		train	turn		drip	dirt
track	term		brow	burn		brand	bird

14.3 R or a Spelling of /er/?

Read the words. Draw a line between the syllables As you read them, compare the vowel sounds.

person   prepay   furnish   frighten

turbo   trumpet   triplet   turnip

14.4 Spelling Cues

Write a cue word for the spellings of /er/.

er

_____

ir

_____

ur

_____

ear

_____

14.5 Writing the Phonograms

Write the new phonograms five times each and say them aloud.

er _____

ir _____

ur _____

ear _____

14.6 Phonogram Practice

Write the phonograms as your teacher dictates them.

1. _____	6. _____	11. _____	16. _____
2. _____	7. _____	12. _____	17. _____
3. _____	8. _____	13. _____	18. _____
4. _____	9. _____	14. _____	19. _____
5. _____	10. _____	15. _____	20. _____

14.7 Phonogram Bingo

ay	kn	th	ou	ur
wh	er	augh	th	sh
ough	gn	ai	ea	or
ear	igh	ir	ch	oy
oa	aw	oe	ck	ng

er	or	oe	ou	ear
ck	ng	ow	ur	ay
ar	ir	oa	wh	sh
aw	augh	igh	oi	th
tch	kn	gn	oy	ai

er	ur	ir	ear	or
ar	kn	au	igh	wh
ai	ou	oe	aw	ck
augh	oo	gn	ch	oa
ay	ow	th	ough	ee

er	ay	oo	oe	wh
th	ea	oi	ar	igh
ir	ck	sh	oy	oa
ur	ear	ng	or	ch
kn	ow	gn	ee	ai

LIST 14

Spelling Words	Part of Speech	Plural Past Tense
1.		
2.		
3.		
4.		
5.		
6.		
7.		
8.		
9.		
10.		
11.		
12.		
13.		
14.		
15.		

14.8 Proper Nouns

Write the proper first and last names of five people in your class or family.

1. _____

2. _____

3. _____

4. _____

5. _____

14.9 Titles of Respect

Write the abbreviation for each title of respect.

1. _____

2. _____

3. _____

4. _____

14.10 Reading

Read the sentences aloud. Underline the proper nouns.

1. Jill waters the flowers.

2. The songbirds eat the birdseed.

3. Patrick and Ann sail boats.

4. Mr. Carter and Mr. Roberts search the river.

5. The women hear David and Mark laughing.

6. The blackbird hurt its wing.

7. The weather turns cold this week.

8. Grandmother likes reading good books in the winter.

9. The children swim, play, run, and shout.

10. Ellen needs flowers, bread, and eggs.

Extra Practice

14.11 Editing

Find the errors. Rewrite each sentence correctly.

1.   the girl's ears hurt   2

_____

_____

2.   the womin sells flowers cards and gifts.   4

_____

_____

3.   a bird searchs the ground   3

_____

_____

4.   mr. lopez sails the boat.   2

_____

_____

5.   joel needs a warm coat   2

_____

_____

14.12 Identifying Parts of Speech

Answer the questions your teacher asks and mark the parts of speech.

The old woman sells birds.

The children jump.

The girl hears birds.

The boy's ear hurts.

14.13 Possessives

Add an apostrophe to make each phrase correct.

1. a boys ear

2. a girls flowers

3. thirteen womens designs

4. three childrens toys

5. ten teachers books

14.14 Compound Words

Combine the words into compound words.

tug + boat = tugboat

1. sail + boat =

2. sea + bird =

3. bird + bath =

4. song + bird =

5. black + bird =

6. flower + pot =

7. sun + flower =

8. grand + child =

9. congress + woman =

10. watch + dog =

14.15 Dictation

Listen to each sentence as your teacher reads it aloud. Repeat it back. Write it on the lines below.

1. _____

_____

2. _____

_____

3. _____

_____

4. _____

_____

5. _____

_____

6. _____

_____

14.16 Composition

Rewrite each sentence by adding an adjective that answers: what kind, or how many. Use one of the following adjectives, or come up with your own: **great, loud, quick, quiet, rock, gray, black, old, thirteen, three...**

1. Father reads a **book**.

   Father reads a great book.

2. The **children** jump.

3. The woman plays the **music**.

4. The girl feeds the **ducks**.

5. The **birds** sing.

6. The **child** turns the knobs.

Lesson 15

15

15.1 Assessment

Listen to each phrase as your teacher dictates. Repeat it back. Write it on the lines below.

1. _____

_____

2. _____

_____

3. _____

_____

4. _____

_____

5. _____

_____

6. _____

_____

7. _____

_____

8. _____

   _____

9. _____

   _____

10. _____

   _____

   _____

15.2 Reading

Read the sentences.

1. The men agree.

2. The child catches the bird and holds it.

3. The cold sailors reach land.

4. Grandfather coughs.

5. The children design and draw toy cars.

6. Asher pulls, pushes, and turns the knob.

7. Parker starts and Taylor waits.

8. Samantha enjoys swim meets.

9. Hudson knows the signs.

10. The loud sound destroys the song.

11. Mother whispers a secret.

12. Father pounds the nail.

13. Touch the ball and pass it on.

14. Quinn wants and needs sleep.

15. The socks match.

16. School starts at three o'clock.

17. The students think.

15.3 Words to Practice

Mark the spelling words which need more practice.

1. ___ agree	21. ___ help	41. ___ search
2. ___ bird	22. ___ hold	42. ___ sell
3. ___ call	23. ___ hurt	43. ___ shout
4. ___ catch	24. ___ jump	44. ___ sign
5. ___ child	25. ___ know	45. ___ sing
6. ___ cold	26. ___ match	46. ___ sleep
7. ___ cough	27. ___ meet	47. ___ start
8. ___ design	28. ___ need	48. ___ talk
9. ___ destroy	29. ___ old	49. ___ teach
10. ___ draw	30. ___ open	50. ___ think
11. ___ drink	31. ___ pass	51. ___ thirteen
12. ___ ear	32. ___ pick	52. ___ throw
13. ___ eat	33. ___ play	53. ___ touch
14. ___ enjoy	34. ___ pound	54. ___ turn
15. ___ fight	35. ___ pull	55. ___ wait
16. ___ find	36. ___ push	56. ___ walk
17. ___ flower	37. ___ reach	57. ___ want
18. ___ follow	38. ___ read	58. ___ watch
19. ___ girl	39. ___ remember	59. ___ whisper
20. ___ hear	40. ___ sail	60. ___ woman

15.4 Adding the Suffix -Ful

Add the suffix -Ful to each of the words.

cup + ful = cupful

1. pain + ful =
2. mouth + ful =
3. glass + ful =
4. spoon + ful =
5. teaspoon + ful =
6. watch + ful =
7. joy + ful =
8. law + ful =
9. event + ful =
10. thought + ful =

15.5 Subject-Verb Agreement

Add -S or -ES if needed to make the subject and verb agree.

1.   The child turn _____ the wheel.

2.   The woman read _____ the newspaper.

3.   The bird search_____ for seeds.

4.   The dog's ears hear_____.

5.   Girls jump _____.

6.   The sailor sing _____ songs

7.   The teacher start _____ the class.

8.   Father pass_____ the sign.

9.   Grandpa pull _____ the string.

10. Mother hold _____ the flower.

15.6 Sentences

Rewrite the sentences with a capital letter and end mark.

the girls know the secret

_____

_____

an old woman watches the birds

_____

_____

the child catches the ball

_____

_____

the girls and boys draw designs

_____

_____

15.7 Sentences and Fragments

Write an S next to the complete sentences. Write F next to the fragments.

1. _____ The boy remembers the man.

2. _____ The old woman.

3. _____ Thirteen sons and daughters.

4. _____ Ella knows the best music.

5. _____ Harper searches the backyard.

6. _____ The children open the door.

7. _____ Flowers.

8. _____ Grandpa drinks the milk.

9. _____ Students like the book.

10. _____ Eat, drink, play, and swim.

15.8 Possessives

Write S for singluar possessives and P for plural possessives.

1. _____ the man's coat

2. _____ Mothers' Day

3. _____ the worker's phone

4. _____ the rescuers' tools

5. _____ the teacher's classroom

6. _____ the players' balls

7. _____ the authors' book

8. _____ the store's prices

9. _____ the boy's cough

10. _____ the skaters' skates

15.9 Commas in a Series

Add a comma to each place it is needed in the sentence.

1. The workers teachers and students eat lunch.

2. The daughters sing shout and play.

3. The girls walk talk and laugh.

4. The students eat bread drink milk and wash the dishes.

15.10 Phonogram Quiz

Write the phonograms as your teacher dictates them.

1. _____	15. _____	29. _____	43. _____
2. _____	16. _____	30. _____	44. _____
3. _____	17. _____	31. _____	45. _____
4. _____	18. _____	32. _____	46. _____
5. _____	19. _____	33. _____	47. _____
6. _____	20. _____	34. _____	48. _____
7. _____	21. _____	35. _____	49. _____
8. _____	22. _____	36. _____	50. _____
9. _____	23. _____	37. _____	51. _____
10. _____	24. _____	38. _____	52. _____
11. _____	25. _____	39. _____	53. _____
12. _____	26. _____	40. _____	54. _____
13. _____	27. _____	41. _____	55. _____
14. _____	28. _____	42. _____	56. _____

15.11 Phonogram Tic-Tac-Toe

Write in the phonograms which need practice randomly on the boards. Play phonogram tic-tac-toe.

Lesson 16

16

16.1 Writing the Phonograms

Write the new phonograms five times each and say them aloud.

ew _____

ed _____

16.2 Phonogram Quiz

Write the phonograms as your teacher dictates them.

1. _____	6. _____	11. _____	16. _____
2. _____	7. _____	12. _____	17. _____
3. _____	8. _____	13. _____	18. _____
4. _____	9. _____	14. _____	19. _____
5. _____	10. _____	15. _____	20. _____

16.3 Single-Letter Vowels

Write the single-letter vowels.

_____   _____   _____

_____   _____

16.4 Single-Letter Consonants

Write the single-letter consonants in alphabetical order.

_____   _____   _____

_____   _____   _____

_____   _____   _____

_____   _____

_____   _____

_____   _____

_____   _____

_____   _____

16.5 C Says /k/

Read the words.

cat	cop	cub	act
cap	cut	clap	picnic

16.6 C Softens to /s/

Read the words. Highlight the E, I or Y.

cent	cell	cinder	cinnamon
center	cinch	citrus	cylinder

16.7 G Says /g/

Read the words.

gap	gum	green	bug
got	glad	big	rag

16.8 G Softens to /j/

Read the words. Highlight the E, I or Y.

gem	ginger	gym
general	margin	gymnast

16.9 G Says /g/

Read the words. Highlight the E, I or Y.

get	gift	argyle

LIST 16

Spelling Words	Part of Speech	Plural Past Tense
1.		
2.		
3.		
4.		
5.		
6.		
7.		
8.		
9.		
10.		
11.		
12.		
13.		
14.		
15.		

16.10 Past Tense

Write the past tense word in the correct column as your teacher says the word and writes it on the board.

/ĕd/	/d/	/t/	Irregular
_____	_____	_____	_____
_____	_____	_____	_____
_____	_____	_____	_____
_____	_____	_____	_____
_____	_____	_____	_____

Extra Practice

16.11 Past Tense Sentences

Rewrite each sentence in the past tense.

1. The woman waters the garden.

   The woman watered the garden.

2. Father pours the milk.

   _____

3. Mother owns a black coat.

   _____

4. The children jump.

   _____

5. The man searches the car.

   _____

16.12 Irregular Past Tense

Complete the sentences with a past tense verb.

heard	grew	met	sang
held	fought	read	found

1. Mother _____ carrots in the garden.

2. Father _____ a new book.

3. The boys _____ loud music.

4. The girl _____ the small cat in her hands.

5. The students _____ a song.

6. Grandpa _____ the lost dog.

7. The children _____ the new teacher.

8. The brothers and sisters _____ over the toys.

16.13 Irregular Past Tense Game

Provide each student with a game piece and die. The first student rolls the die and advances the number of spaces shown. As he passes each verb, he must read it aloud and state the past tense form. If the student misses one, he must remain on that space until the next turn. If a 3 is rolled, he must go back to start. Optional: The students are required to say a sentence using the past tense verb.

START	STOP
get	think
see	teach
catch	tell
draw	sing
drink	begin
fight	blow
eat	fall
find	feed
hold	go
know	grind
meet	hang
read	grow
sell	keep
sleep	light

16.14 Irregular Past Tense

Fill in the chart with the past tense form of each verb.

Present Tense	Past Tense
grow	
get	
see	
catch	
draw	
drink	
fight	
find	
hear	
hold	
know	
meet	
read	

16.15 Identifying Parts of Speech

Mark the parts of speech in each of the sentences while your teacher marks them on the board.

Grandmother watered the flowers.

Anna's father saw a wonderful program.

Rebecca got a new winter coat and new shoes.

16.16 Reading

Read the sentences aloud.

1. The farmer grew sunflowers.

2. An eraser costs fifteen cents.

3. Sam needs new shoes.

4. The children learned a lesson.

5. The bird has a hurt wing.

6. The girls picked the flowers.

7. Children designed the birthday card.

8. He rode the bike.

9. Father owns a green truck.

10. Great-grandmother poured the water on the plants.

16.17 Dictation

Listen to each sentence as your teacher reads it aloud. Repeat it back. Write it on the lines below.

1. _____

_____

2. _____

_____

3. _____

_____

4. _____

_____

5. _____

_____

6. _____

_____

16.18 Composition

Write 6 sentences with a subject, past tense verb, and direct object. Make sure to change the verb from present tense to past tense.

children	drink	hill
mother	pour	cliff
author	see	book
worker	need	oil
writer	pick	milk
aunt	sign	paper
son	mail	wheel
boy	pull	water
	hold	gift

Six children drank water.

1. _____

2. _____

3. _____

4. _____

5. _____

6. _____

16.19 The Prefix UN-

Combine the prefix -un and the past tense to form new words.

1.	~~attended~~	5.	owned	9.	needed
2.	known	6.	caught	10.	heard
3.	signed	7.	taught		
4.	matched	8.	touched		

1. _unattended_

2. _____

3. _____

4. _____

5. _____

6. _____

7. _____

8. _____

9. _____

10. _____

Lesson 17

17.1 The Phonogram UI

Read the words. Underline the UI.

fruit   suit   recruit

ruin   pursuit

17.2 Writing the Phonograms

Write the new phonogram five times and say it aloud.

ui

17.3 Phonogram Practice

Write the phonograms as your teacher dictates them.

1. _____   6. _____   11. _____   16. _____

2. _____   7. _____   12. _____   17. _____

3. _____   8. _____   13. _____   18. _____

4. _____   9. _____   14. _____   19. _____

5. _____   10. _____   15. _____   20. _____

17.4 The Vowel Sound Changes Because of the E

Write the words as your teacher dictates them.

_____   _____

_____   _____

_____   _____

_____   _____

_____   _____

17.5 Word Search

Create a word search using the words provided by your teacher.

17.6 The Long /ū/ Sound

A E O U usually say their names at the end of the syllable.	The vowel says its name because of the E.
_____	_____
_____	_____
_____	_____
_____	_____
_____	_____

LIST 17

Spelling Words	Part of Speech	Plural Past Tense
1.		
2.		
3.		
4.		
5.		
6.		
7.		
8.		
9.		
10.		
11.		
12.		
13.		
14.		
15.		

17.7 Identifying Parts of Speech

Mark the parts of speech in each of the sentences while your teacher marks them on the board.

Ava got a wonderful birthday gift.

The children celebrated Carter's birthday.

The careful boy hid the old shoes.

17.8 Quotations

Read each sentence aloud. Circle the comma and quotation marks. Underline the capital letter.

1.   Sam said, "Taylor hid the book."

2.   "Taylor hid the book," said Sam.

3.   Father said, "Mother watered the flowers."

4.   "Mother watered the flowers," said Father.

5.   Mother said, "Matt grew five inches."

6.   "Matt grew five inches," said Mother.

17.9 Consonant and Vowel Suffixes

Circle the vowel suffixes.

-est	-ing	-ness	-en
-ly	-ed	-ful	-ist
-ment	-able	-er	-ship

17.10 Adding Suffixes to Silent Final E Words

Add the ending to each word.

1. shine + ed =

2. care + ful =

3. state + s =

4. type + ist =

5. name + ed =

6. use + less =

7. use + ed =

8. name + less =

9. hope + ful =

10. hope + ed =

11. name + s =

12. ride + er =

17.11 Additional Spelling

17.12 Reading

Read the sentences aloud.

1. The sisters share a bedroom.

2. He celebrated his birthday at the pool.

3. King Richard ruled from 1189 - 1199.

4. The teacher said, "The class begins at ten o'clock."

5. The children ate sandwiches, apples, and fruit.

6. Thirteen fish swam in the tank.

7. The teacher showed the students the lesson.

8. The boys read good books in class.

9. The dog hid his large bone in the yard.

10. The sun shines.

17.13 Dictation

Listen to each sentence as your teacher reads it aloud. Repeat it back. Write it on the lines below.

1. _____

_____

2. _____

_____

3. _____

_____

4. _____

_____

5. _____

_____

6. _____

_____

17.14 Composition

Rewrite each sentence by adding an adjective that answers: what kind, or how many. Use one of the following adjectives, or come up with your own: **quiet, loud, high, low, black, green, white, sharp, ...**

1. The boys played a **game**.

   The boys played a quiet game.

2. The children used the **swing**.

3. The girls hid the **toy**.

4. The woman named the **cat**.

5. The brothers used the **tools**.

Lesson 18

18.1 Writing the Phonograms

Write the new phonograms five times each and say them aloud.

wor _____

wr _____

18.2 Phonogram Practice

Write the phonograms as your teacher dictates them.

1. _____	6. _____	11. _____	16. _____
2. _____	7. _____	12. _____	17. _____
3. _____	8. _____	13. _____	18. _____
4. _____	9. _____	14. _____	19. _____
5. _____	10. _____	15. _____	20. _____

18.3 WR and WOR

Read the words. Underline the phonograms WR and WOR.

wrap	word
wrath	work
wreck	world
write	worm
wrote	worship
wring	worst
wrong	worth

18.4 Silent Final E

Read each word and mark the reason for the silent final E.

have	give	curve	weave
live	mauve	olive	serve

18.5 Silent Final E

Read each word and mark the reason for the silent final E.

clue	glue	argue	value
blue	true	due	cue

18.6 English Words Do Not End in V or U

Practice spelling the words as your teacher reads them.

1. _____

2. _____

3. _____

4. _____

5. _____

18.7 Silent Final E

Read each word and mark the reason for the silent final E.

grace   rice   voice   trace

mice   face   sauce   dance

18.8 Silent Final E

Read each word and mark the reason for the silent final E.

large   huge   orange   surge

page   stage   strange   age

18.9 The C says /s/ and the G says /j/ because of the E

Practice spelling the words as your teacher reads them.

1. _____

2. _____

3. _____

4. _____

5. _____

LIST 18

Spelling Words	Part of Speech	Plural Past Tense
1.		
2.		
3.		
4.		
5.		
6.		
7.		
8.		
9.		
10.		
11.		
12.		
13.		
14.		
15.		

18.10 Identifying Parts of Speech

Read the sentences. Mark the parts of speech.

The teacher gave the boy an apple.

The boy gave the teacher an apple.

The girl told the woman a secret.

The woman told the girl a secret.

18.11 Adding Suffixes to Silent Final E Words

Add the ending to each word.

1. ride + er = _____

2. table + s = _____

3. care + less = _____

4. care + ful = _____

5. write + er = _____

6. type + ist = _____

7. move + er = _____

18.12 Irregular Past Tense Verbs

Draw lines to match the present and past tense verbs.

1.	told	sleep
2.	got	eat
3.	saw	drink
4.	caught	see
5.	drew	catch
6.	drank	get
7.	fought	draw
8.	ate	write
9.	found	tell
10.	held	fight
11.	knew	keep
12.	kept	find
13.	read	hold
14.	sold	know
15.	slept	sell
16.	wrote	read

18.13 Quotes

Add commas and quotation marks where needed to each sentence.

1. The teacher said it is time to start the class.

2. The show starts at five o'clock said the clerk.

3. Mrs Hammel said read chapters three and four today.

4. We love ice cream shouted the children.

18.14 Reading

Read the sentences aloud.

1. The dog jumps the fence.

2. Mother wants a black coat, a green handbag, and a brown dress.

3. The teacher read the children a great book.

4. The students, teachers, mothers, and fathers all enjoyed the program.

5. The author writes books, types papers, and reads the mail.

6. The boy plays baseball, skates, and swims.

7. The woman showed her daughter the new shoes.

8. The players bring bats, balls, and gloves.

9. Grandmother wrote Tim a long letter.

10. He offered her ten dollars.

18.15 Dictation

Listen to each sentence as your teacher reads it aloud. Repeat it back. Write it on the lines below.

1. _____

_____

2. _____

_____

3. _____

_____

4. _____

_____

5. _____

_____

6. _____

_____

18.16 Composition

Write a simple sentence.

_____

Ask four questions to add detail to your sentence. Each time rewrite the sentence with the answer.

1. _____

   _____

2. _____

   _____

3. _____

   _____

4. _____

   _____

18.17 Adding Prefixes

Add the prefixes to the words. Use them in a sentence out loud.

1. mis + take = _____

2. mis + lead = _____

3. mis + trust = _____

4. mis + used = _____

5. mis + calculate = _____

6. over + take = _____

7. over + due = _____

8. over + flow = _____

9. over + night = _____

10. under + stand = _____

11. under + sized = _____

12. under + paid = _____

Lesson 19

19.1 The Phonogram PH

Read each of the words aloud. Underline the PH.

graph   phrase   phone

photo   pharmacist   telephone

photograph   phonogram

19.2 Writing the Phonograms

Write the new phonogram five times and say it aloud.

ph _____

19.3 Phonogram Practice

Write the phonograms as your teacher dictates them.

1. _____   6. _____   11. _____   16. _____

2. _____   7. _____   12. _____   17. _____

3. _____   8. _____   13. _____   18. _____

4. _____   9. _____   14. _____   19. _____

5. _____   10. _____   15. _____   20. _____

19.4 Every Syllable Needs a Vowel

Read the words. Underline the final syllable.

double	middle	buckle	title
trouble	sniffle	pickle	settle
uncle	waffle	apple	puzzle
candle	wiggle	maple	sizzle
cradle	eagle	hassle	

19.5 Final Syllable

Write the 10 syllables that end in -le.

1. _____   4. _____   7. _____   10. _____

2. _____   5. _____   8. _____

3. _____   6. _____   9. _____

19.6 Syllables and Vowels

Read the words. Write a / between the syllables.

table	middle	twinkle	title
bubble	waffle	apple	puzzle
uncle	wiggle	maple	
cradle	eagle	hassle	

19.7 Silent Final E

Read the words. Underline the reason for the silent final E once and underline the silent final E twice.

house	horse	promise
mouse	goose	license
spouse	moose	cause

LIST 19

Spelling Words	Part of Speech	Plural Past Tense
1.		
2.		
3.		
4.		
5.		
6.		
7.		
8.		
9.		
10.		
11.		
12.		
13.		
14.		
15.		

19.8 Simple Subject and Simple Predicate

Write the simple subject and simple predicate to form the simple sentence.

1. David gave me a wonderful photograph.

   David gave.

2. The farmer grew apples.

   _____

3. Thirteen children celebrated Emma's birthday.

   _____

4. Mom likes the blue phone.

   _____

5. The large dog brought dad a ball.

   _____

19.9 Identifying Parts of Speech

Read the sentences. Mark the parts of speech while your teacher writes them on the board.

The large horse pulled the hay wagon.

The kind teacher offered the children apple juice.

The photographer moved six little tables.

Extra Practice

19.10 Articles

Write the correct article "a" or "an" before each phrase.

1. _____ old flowerpot

2. _____ little table

3. _____ large house

4. _____ open door

5. _____ enjoyable game

19.11 Titles of Respect

Write the abbreviation for each title of respect.

1. _____

2. _____

3. _____

4. _____

19.12 Reading

Read the sentences aloud.

1. The groom offered the horse an apple.

2. We celebrated Grandmother's birthday last week.

3. The little boy drank apple juice for lunch.

4. Mother moved the large table.

5. The children liked the gifts.

6. Father changed the design.

7. Three girls remembered the answer.

8. We heard laughter in the other room.

9. The wind blew the trees.

10. The man said, "The boys had a wonderful time at the program."

19.13 Adding the Suffix -able

Add the suffix -able to each of these words.

work	reach	trace	agree
change	solve	save	
value	enjoy	charge	

1. *workable*

2. _____

3. _____

4. _____

5. _____

6. _____

7. _____

8. _____

9. _____

10. _____

19.14 Dictation

Listen to each sentence as your teacher reads it aloud. Repeat it back. Write it on the lines below.

1. _____

_____

2. _____

_____

3. _____

_____

4. _____

_____

5. _____

_____

6. _____

_____

19.15 Composition

Write a simple sentence.

_____

Ask four questions to add detail to your sentence. Each time rewrite the sentence with the answer.

1. _____

2. _____

3. _____

   _____

4. _____

   _____

Lesson 20

20.1 Assessment

Listen to each phrase as your teacher dictates. Repeat it back. Write it on the lines below.

1. _____

_____

2. _____

_____

3. _____

_____

4. _____

_____

5. _____

_____

6. _____

_____

7. _____

_____

8. _____

_____

9. _____

_____

10. _____

_____

20.2 Reading

Read the sentences.

1. The boys attended class and learned useful new words.

2. The sun shines.

3. Mother and Father celebrated.

4. The girls saw the blue shoes.

5. Bring the suit and shoes.

6. the horse's new name

7. The boy grew three inches.

8. Father said, "Write the letter."

9. say, says, said

10. Mother said, "Save the change."

11. Bring a coat, shoes, and warm socks.

12. ten cents

13. Get a ride.

14. Share the toys.

15. bad germs

16. The children hide.

17. The girls traced the trees.

18. Spell the words.

19. United States, Canada, and The United Kingdom

20. the children's lessons

20.3 Words to Practice

Mark the spelling words which need more practice.

1. ___ answer	22. ___ learn	43. ___ see
2. ___ apple	23. ___ lesson	44. ___ share
3. ___ attend	24. ___ letter	45. ___ shine
4. ___ birthday	25. ___ like	46. ___ shoe
5. ___ blue	26. ___ little	47. ___ show
6. ___ bring	27. ___ love	48. ___ spell
7. ___ celebrate	28. ___ make	49. ___ state
8. ___ cents	29. ___ move	50. ___ suit
9. ___ change	30. ___ name	51. ___ table
10. ___ excellent	31. ___ new	52. ___ take
11. ___ fruit	32. ___ offer	53. ___ tell
12. ___ germs	33. ___ own	54. ___ trace
13. ___ get	34. ___ phone	55. ___ use
14. ___ gift	35. ___ photograph	56. ___ water
15. ___ give	36. ___ pour	57. ___ wonderful
16. ___ grow	37. ___ ride	58. ___ word
17. ___ hide	38. ___ rule	59. ___ work
18. ___ horse	39. ___ said	60. ___ write
19. ___ house	40. ___ save	
20. ___ juice	41. ___ say	
21. ___ large	42. ___ says	

20.4 Sink & Spell

	1	2	3	4	5	6	7	8	9	10	11	12	13	14	15	16	17
A																	
B																	
C																	
D																	
E																	
F																	
G																	
H																	
I																	
J																	
K																	
L																	
M																	
N																	

20.5 **Silent Final E Game**

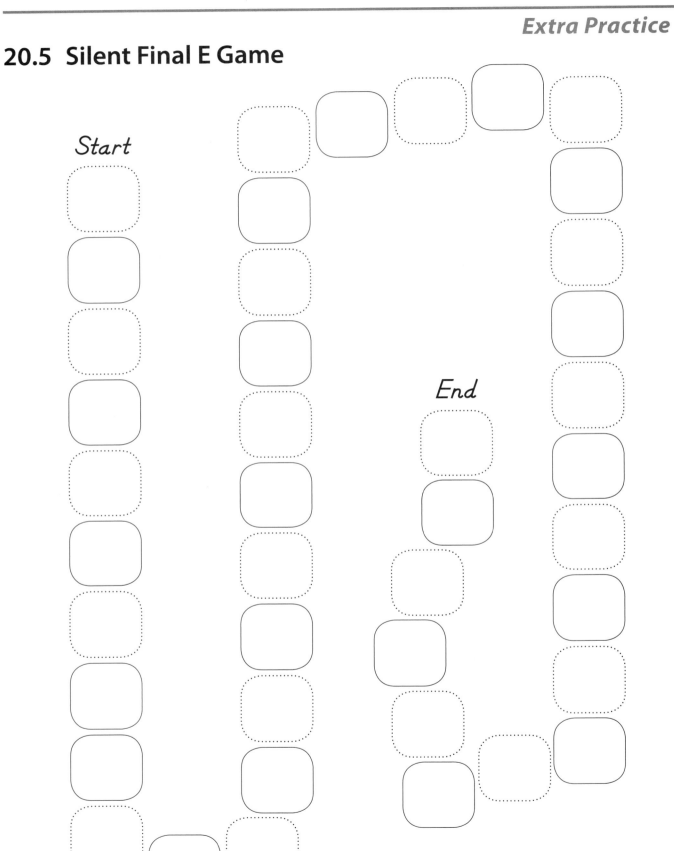

Start

End

20.6 ED Past Tense Ending

Write the words in the correct column as your teacher reads them.

/ĕd/	/d/	/t/
_____	_____	_____
_____	_____	_____
_____	_____	_____
_____	_____	_____
_____	_____	_____
_____	_____	_____
_____	_____	_____
_____	_____	_____
_____	_____	_____
_____	_____	_____

20.7 Irregular Verbs

Match the present tense and past tense verbs.

~~brought~~	took	grew	rode	held
knew	sold	sang	slept	found
saw	caught	ate	heard	
met	gave	hid	taught	
got	threw	fought	said	
read	drew	made	thought	

1. bring *brought*

2. get

3. give

4. grow

5. hide

6. make

7. ride

8. say

9. see

10. take

11. catch

12. draw

13. eat

14. fight

15. find

16. hear

17. hold

18. know

19. meet

20. read

21. sell

22. sing

23. sleep

24. teach

25. think

26. throw

20.8 Phonogram Quiz

Write the phonograms as your teacher dictates them.

1. ___17___	___33.___	___49.___	_____
2. _____	18. _____	34._____	50._____
3. _____	19. _____	35._____	51. _____
4. _____	20._____	36._____	52._____
5. _____	21. _____	37._____	53._____
6. _____	22. _____	38._____	54._____
7. _____	23. _____	39._____	55._____
8. _____	24._____	40._____	56._____
9. _____	25._____	41. _____	57._____
10._____	26._____	42._____	58._____
11. _____	27._____	43._____	59._____
12._____	28._____	44._____	60._____
13._____	29._____	45._____	
14._____	30._____	46._____	
15._____	31. _____	47._____	
16._____	32._____	48._____	

20.9 Phonogram Flip

1	
2	
3	
4	
5	
6	
7	
8	
9	
10	
11	
12	

Lesson 21

21.1 Reading Words with EI

Read the words. Underline the EI.

/ā/	/ē/	/ī/
their	weird	(either)
reign	either	(neither)
veil	neither	seismic
vein	leisure	kaleidoscope
heir	protein	rottweiler
skein	seize	Einstein
surveillance	caffeine	feisty
	sheik	

21.2 Reading Words with EY

/ā/	/ē/	
they	honey	turkey
hey	hockey	valley
obey	alley	volley
convey	money	chimney
prey	kidney	donkey
whey	pulley	monkey
	parsley	jersey

21.3 Reading Words with EIGH

/ā/	/ī/
eight	height
freight	sleight
sleigh	
weigh	
neigh	
neighbor	

21.4 Writing The Phonograms

Write the new phonograms five times each and say them aloud.

ei

ey

eigh

21.5 Phonogram Practice

Write the phonograms as your teacher dictates them.

1. _____	6. _____	11. _____	16. _____
2. _____	7. _____	12. _____	17. _____
3. _____	8. _____	13. _____	18. _____
4. _____	9. _____	14. _____	19. _____
5. _____	10. _____	15. _____	20. _____

Extra Practice

21.6 Silent Final E Game

Cut out the cards. Place them face down on the table. Choose a card, read it, and identify the reason(s) for the silent final E.

- If you read the word correctly and identify all the reasons for the silent E, keep the card.

- If you cannot read the word or miss one of the reasons, the card is returned to the pile.

- If you draw one of the additional cards, you should follow the directions on the card. These cards are not returned to the pile once they are used, but set aside.

- Play ends when all the cards are drawn.

Award points as follows:

- one point for reading the word correctly

- one point for identifying each reason for the silent final E

- one point for each card in your possession at the end of the game

The person with the most points wins.

Return 2 Cards	Return 1 Card
Loose 2 points	**Loose 5 points**
Add 2 points	**Add 2 points**
Add 5 points	**Add 1 point**

flute	rule
whole	cube
mule	eve
forgive	native
prove	survive
avenue	continue
glue	curve
ice	fence
peace	hinge
change	orange
moose	mouse
house	purse

LIST 21

Spelling Words	Part of Speech	Plural Past Tense
1.		
2.		
3.		
4.		
5.		
6.		
7.		
8.		
9.		
10.		
11.		
12.		
13.		
14.		
15.		

21.7 Subject Pronouns

Write the subject pronouns.

Subject Pronouns
_____
_____
_____
_____
_____
_____

21.8 Identifying Parts of Speech

Read the sentences. Mark the parts of speech while your teacher writes them on the board.

We ate breakfast.

She practiced the difficult music.

He added the large numbers.

They weighed the apples and the oranges.

I read the little boy a good book.

21.9 Matching the Pronoun to the Person

Match the pronouns to the person.

I	he	it	we
you	she	they	

First Person   _____   _____

Second Person   _____

Third Person   _____   _____   _____   _____

21.10 First, Second, or Third Person

Read each short story. Is it told in first, second, or third person? Circle the answer.

Father went to the store. He picked eight perfect apples. He weighed them on the scale. Then he paid for them. The apples cost seven dollars.

first person   second person   third person

I saw a wild raccoon in my yard. I ran and got a camera. I took photos of the raccoon and mailed them to Grandmother.

first person   second person   third person

You ate lunch at Mrs. Allen's house. You had chicken, salad, cake, and milk. When you finished you said, "Thank you for the wonderful lunch."

first person   third person
second person

21.11 Subject Pronouns

Rewrite each sentence by substituting a subject pronoun for the word in bold.

Mrs. Young made dinner.

She made dinner.

_____

The men weighed the fish.

_____

_____

Parker typed the paper.

_____

_____

The dog weighed six pounds.

_____

_____

Abigail, Owen, and Nolan washed the clothes.

_____

_____

21.12 Articles

Write the correct article *a* or *an* before each phrase.

1. _____ old flowerpot

2. _____ great lunch

3. _____ good weight

4. _____ open door

5. _____ wild duck

21.13 Titles of Respect

Rewrite the name using an abbreviation for the title of respect.

Mister Hansen _____ *Mr. Hansen* _____

Miss Andrea Davis _____

Doctor Wright _____

Misses Paige Miller _____

Extra Practice

21.14 Reading

Read the sentences aloud.

1. I photographed the wild horses.

2. They ate eight apples, three oranges, and five bananas for a snack.

3. She typed the letters on the computer.

4. We practiced the lesson.

5. She added the numbers.

6. You spelled the words right.

7. He ate breakfast and lunch with Mr. and Mrs. Jones.

8. You moved the little table.

9. I enjoyed dinner.

10. It rang three times.

21.15 Dictation

Listen to each sentence as your teacher reads it aloud. Repeat it back. Write it on the lines below.

1. _____

_____

2. _____

_____

3. _____

_____

4. _____

_____

5. _____

_____

6. _____

_____

21.16 Composition

Write sentences using first, second, and third person.

First person

_____

_____

Second person

_____

_____

Third person

_____

_____

_____

Lesson 22

22.1 Phonogram Practice

Write the phonograms as your teacher dictates them.

1. _____
2. _____
3. _____
4. _____
5. _____

6. _____
7. _____
8. _____
9. _____
10. _____

11. _____
12. _____
13. _____
14. _____
15. _____

16. _____
17. _____
18. _____
19. _____
20. _____

22.2 Silent Final E

Read the words. Underline the silent final E twice.

are   axe   rye

awe   dye   bye

22.3 Silent Final E

Read the words. Underline the silent final E twice.

bath bathe   breath breathe

cloth clothe   teeth teethe

22.4 Silent Final E

Read the words. Underline the silent final E twice.

brows browse   laps lapse

teas tease   or ore

22.5 Silent Final E Game

Cut out the cards. Place them face down on the table. Choose a card, read it, and identify the reason(s) for the silent final E.

- If you read the word correctly and identify all the reasons for the silent E, keep the card.

- If you cannot read the word or miss one of the reasons, the card is returned to the pile.

- If you draw one of the additional cards, you should follow the directions on the card. These cards are not returned to the pile once they are used, but set aside.

- Play ends when all the cards are drawn.

Award points as follows:

- one point for reading the word correctly

- one point for identifying each reason for the silent final E

- one point for each card in your possession at the end of the game

The person with the most points wins.

Return 5 Card	**Return 2 Cards**
Loose 2 points	**Loose 5 points**
Add 5 points	**Add 2 points**

come	some
done	were
are	whole
owe	peace
bathe	tease
teethe	style
race	cage
cake	pave
whale	mile
battle	circle
maple	noodle
quote	chore

LIST 22

Spelling Words	Part of Speech	Plural Past Tense
1.		
2.		
3.		
4.		
5.		
6.		
7.		
8.		
9.		
10.		
11.		
12.		
13.		
14.		
15.		

22.6 Object Pronouns

Write the subject pronouns and the object pronouns.

Subject Pronouns	Object Pronouns

22.7 Identifying Parts of Speech

Write the parts of speech as your teacher identifies them on the board.

We fought it.

They saw him.

The firemen rescued her.

I gave him the ball.

She sold them three books.

22.8 Pronouns

Fill in a pronoun that completes each sentence.

1. *The author sold* _____ *six books.*

2. *Mother told* _____ *the secret.*

3. _____ *shared the toys.*

4. _____ *made Grandmother a hat.*

5. *The students liked* _____.

6. _____ *made the girl a birthday cake.*

7. *Ellen brought* _____ *water.*

8. _____ *hid the gift.*

9. _____ *wrote* _____ *a letter.*

10. _____ *practiced the music.*

Extra Practice

22.9 Sentences and Fragments

Write S for sentence and F for fragment.

1. _____ We met the workers.

2. _____ They saw us.

3. _____ Seven likable students.

4. _____ Rescued the dog.

5. _____ Simple clothes.

6. _____ The girl took them.

22.10 Person

Read each short story. Is it told in first, second, or third person? Circle the answer.

I went home, found my old clothes and changed. I wanted to work in the garden. I planted six beautiful flowers.

first person   second person   third person

The students were happy. They studied hard for the test. When they took the test, they all got perfect scores.

first person   second person   third person

You helped watch the baby while Mrs. Johnson made dinner. When the baby cried, you fed her. You played with her and sang songs to the her.

first person   second person   third person

22.11 Editing

Each sentence includes three mistakes. Rewrite each one without the mistakes.

the littl boy rescueed the black cat.

_____

_____

mom gav him the nife.

_____

_____

bring warm clothes boots and a hat.

_____

_____

22.12 Reading

Read the sentences aloud.

1. Mom came home at ten o'clock.

2. We live in a yellow house.

3. I gave her a simple white dress.

4. He took them home.

5. They told us the price.

6. He weighed the puppy.

7. The puppy weighed eight pounds.

8. We practiced the song.

9. I brought some paper.

10. She loves the blue flowers.

22.13 Composition

Write 6 sentences with a subject pronoun, past tense verb, object pronoun.

I	guessed	me
you	saw	you
he	needed	him
she	picked	her
it	copied	it
we	used	us
they	met	them

1. _____

2. _____

3. _____

4. _____

5. _____

6. _____

22.14 Dictation

Listen to each sentence as your teacher reads it aloud. Repeat it back. Write it on the lines below.

1. _____

_____

2. _____

_____

3. _____

_____

4. _____

_____

5. _____

_____

6. _____

_____

22.15 Compound Words

Combine the words to form ten new compound words.

home	apple	back	cat
key	pass	board	pad
white	farm	sauce	knife
pocket	bird	sick	fire
wild	light	work	room
come	house	word	

1. _____

2. _____

3. _____

4. _____

5. _____

6. _____

7. _____

8. _____

9. _____

10. _____

Lesson 23

23

23.1 The Phonograms BU and GU

Read the words. Underline the BU and the GU.

build   guilt

built   guide

buy   guard

buoyant   guitar

                               guy

                               guarantee

                               guess

                               guest

                               tongue

23.2 Writing the Phonograms

Write the new phonograms five times each and say them aloud.

bu _____

gu _____

23.3 Phonogram Blitz

23.4 The Sounds of Y

Write the three vowel sounds of Y.

_____   _____   _____

23.5 Y at the End of the Word

Write the words as your teacher writes them on the board.

/ĭ/	/ī/	/ē/
_____	_____	_____
_____	_____	_____
_____	_____	_____
_____	_____	_____
_____	_____	_____
_____	_____	_____

LIST 23

Spelling Words	Part of Speech	Plural Past Tense
1.		
2.		
3.		
4.		
5.		
6.		
7.		
8.		
9.		
10.		
11.		
12.		
13.		
14.		
15.		

23.6 Pronouns

Write the pronouns as directed by your teacher.

Subject Pronouns	Object Pronouns	Possessive Pronoun Adjectives
_____	_____	_____
_____	_____	_____
_____	_____	_____
_____	_____	_____
_____	_____	_____
_____	_____	_____
_____	_____	_____

23.7 Identifying Parts of Speech

Write the parts of speech as your teacher identifies them on the board.

We bought his car.

Our students built the rocket.

My brother visited your school.

Their workers guessed the problem.

23.8 Pronouns 1

Rewrite each sentence replacing the word(s) in **bold** with the correct pronoun.

1. The boy guessed **Sam's** name.

_____

_____

2. **My brother and sister** bought new MP3 players.

_____

_____

3. **My sisters'** bedrooms are upstairs.

_____

_____

4. My grandparents built **my grandparents'** house in 1953.

_____

_____

5. The students visited **Mrs. Maple** in the hospital.

_____

_____

23.9 Pronouns 2

Fill in the pronoun(s) that completes each sentence.

1. _____ gave the baby a toy.

2. _____ heard _____ loud cry.

3. _____ shared the toys.

4. The teacher gave _____ a prize.

5. _____ visited my grandmother last weekend.

6. _____ wrote _____ a letter.

7. _____ bought _____ a gift.

8. _____ birthday is on Sunday.

9. _____ guessed the answer.

10. _____ threw the coach the basketball.

Extra Practice

23.10 Editing

Each sentence includes four mistakes. Rewrite each one without the mistakes.

i gav her the wite clothes

_____

_____

she cam hom

_____

_____

the students teachers and parents built the new playground

_____

_____

the happee babee plays

_____

_____

_____

23.11 Adding Suffixes to Single Vowel Y Words

Write the new word.

1. cry + ing = _____

2. dry + ed = _____

3. hungry + ly = _____

4. study + ed = _____

5. study + ing = _____

6. copy + ed = _____

7. baby + ish = _____

8. happy + ness = _____

9. buy + ing = _____

10. hungry + er = _____

23.12 Plurals

Write the plural of each word.

1. *baby* _____

2. *puppy* _____

3. *day* _____

4. *toy* _____

5. *lady* _____

6. *key* _____

7. *hobby* _____

8. *sky* _____

9. *monkey* _____

23.13 Adding Suffixes Flow Chart

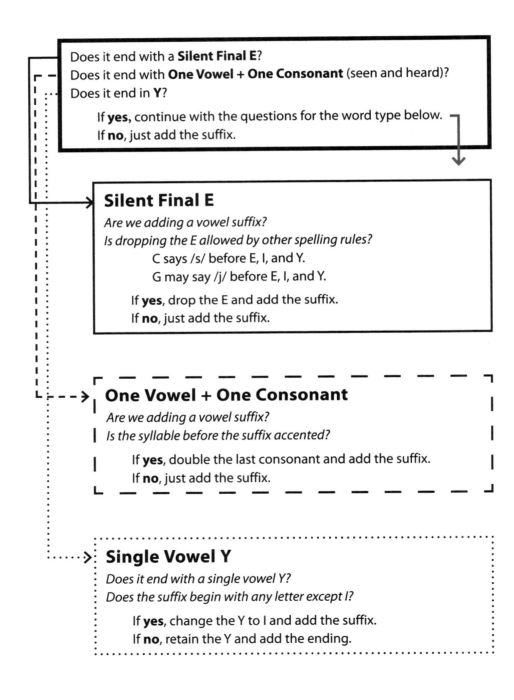

Does it end with a **Silent Final E**?
Does it end with **One Vowel + One Consonant** (seen and heard)?
Does it end in **Y**?

 If **yes**, continue with the questions for the word type below.
 If **no**, just add the suffix.

Silent Final E

Are we adding a vowel suffix?
Is dropping the E allowed by other spelling rules?
 C says /s/ before E, I, and Y.
 G may say /j/ before E, I, and Y.

 If **yes**, drop the E and add the suffix.
 If **no**, just add the suffix.

One Vowel + One Consonant

Are we adding a vowel suffix?
Is the syllable before the suffix accented?

 If **yes**, double the last consonant and add the suffix.
 If **no**, just add the suffix.

Single Vowel Y

Does it end with a single vowel Y?
Does the suffix begin with any letter except I?

 If **yes**, change the Y to I and add the suffix.
 If **no**, retain the Y and add the ending.

23.14 Reading

Read the sentences aloud.

1. The young girl happily watched the baby.

2. The students guessed the wrong answers on their test.

3. Eight children attended the birthday party.

4. The whiteboard is dirty.

5. She lost her priceless ring at the park.

6. They played wonderful music on the keyboard.

7. We simplified the program.

8. The overweight dog needs a better diet.

9. They went camping in the wild forest.

10. She never answers her cellphone.

23.15 Dictation

Listen to each sentence as your teacher reads it aloud. Repeat it back. Write it on the lines below.

1. _____

_____

2. _____

_____

3. _____

_____

4. _____

_____

5. _____

_____

6. _____

_____

23.16 Composition

Rewrite the sentences replacing the words in bold with pronouns..

Ella rescued the white cat. **Ella** kept the **cat** as **Ella's** pet and played with the **cat**.

_____

_____

Jacob studied the question. **Jacob** guessed the right answer to the **question**.

_____

_____

23.17 Composition

Write a sentence that uses at least two possessive pronouns.

_____

_____

_____

Lesson 24

24.1 Phonogram Practice

Write the phonograms as your teacher dictates them.

1. _____   6. _____   11. _____   16. _____

2. _____   7. _____   12. _____   17. _____

3. _____   8. _____   13. _____   18. _____

4. _____   9. _____   14. _____   19. _____

5. _____   10. _____   15. _____   20. _____

LIST 24

	Spelling Words	Part of Speech	Plural Past Tense
1.			
2.			
3.			
4.			
5.			
6.			
7.			
8.			
9.			
10.			
11.			
12.			
13.			
14.			
15.			

24.2 Identifying Parts of Speech

Write the parts of speech as your teacher writes them on the board.

The children read silently.

My brother slowly ate the apple.

Yesterday their family built a tree house.

Extra Practice

24.3 Editing

Each sentence includes three mistakes. Rewrite each one without the mistakes.

Mi brothers often guess the rit answer

_____

_____

she carefullee copied the book.

_____

_____

mother accidently burnd the bread

_____

_____

Extra Practice

24.4 Pronouns

Fill in a pronoun that completes each sentence.

1. _____ *often listens to stories before bedtime.*

2. _____ *family gave her beautiful flowers.*

3. *The animals ate* _____ *food quickly.*

4. *Sometimes* _____ *forget my book.*

5. _____ *lifted the heavy boxes carefully.*

6. *The player accidently kicked* _____

7. _____ *brother never listens.*

8. Yesterday   practiced for three hours.

9. The child carelessly threw coat in the mud.

10. An amazing storyteller told the tale.

24.5 The Suffix -LY

Write the new word.

1. large + ly = _____

2. warm + ly = _____

3. heavy + ly = _____

4. secret + ly = _____

5. careful + ly = _____

6. cold + ly = _____

7. night + ly = _____

8. perfect + ly = _____

9. hungry + ly = _____

10. happy + ly = _____

24.6 Reading

Read the sentences aloud.

1. The workers fixed the leak carefully.

2. Six students never read the book.

3. Yesterday five happy children played at the park.

4. The children practiced the game cheerfully.

5. I hungrily ate my dinner.

6. Today the trucks drove crazily down the street.

7. The wild animals walked restlessly around their cages.

8. The boy slowly added the numbers.

9. He never answers the teacher.

10. She played the music beautifully.

24.7 Dictation

Listen to each sentence as your teacher reads it aloud. Repeat it back. Write it on the lines below.

1. _____

   _____

2. _____

   _____

3. _____

   _____

4. _____

   _____

5. _____

   _____

6. _____

   _____

24.8 Composition

Write 5 sentences with a subject, verb, adverb, and direct object.

I	~~attend~~	often	house
workers	sleep	never	number
teachers	wash	carefully	boat
students	study	accidently	party
they	build	quickly	answer
family	guess	perfectly	car
Grandfather	watch	~~every day~~	~~school~~

I attend school every day.

1. _____

   _____

2. _____

   _____

3. _____

   _____

4. _____

   _____

5. _____

   _____

Lesson 25

25.1 Assessment

Listen to each phrase as your teacher dictates. Repeat it back. Write it on the lines below.

1. _____

_____

2. _____

_____

3. _____

_____

4. _____

_____

5. _____

_____

6. _____

_____

7. _____

_____

8. _____

_____

9. _____

_____

10. _____

_____

25.2 Reading

Read the sentences.

1.   The man accidently hurt his finger.

2.   Add the numbers three and four.

3.   The teacher asked.

4.   The students answered.

5.   The worker hauled a heavy load.

6.   The man weighed too much for his height.

7.   I told the happy children simple stories.

8.   Use the sharp knife.

9.   The hungry workers ate lunch.

10. I often study late at night.

11. We rescued their ducks.

12. She slowly and carefully practiced the music.

13. I have some.

14. We gave them a present.

15. I saw a beautiful yellow coat.

16. We celebrated your birthday.

17. The helpers listened carefully.

25.3 Words to Practice

Mark the spelling words which need more practice.

1. ___ accident	21. ___ height	41. ___ some
2. ___ add	22. ___ her	42. ___ sometimes
3. ___ animal	23. ___ home	43. ___ story
4. ___ ask	24. ___ hungry	44. ___ student
5. ___ baby	25. ___ I	45. ___ study
6. ___ beautiful	26. ___ its	46. ___ their
7. ___ breakfast	27. ___ key	47. ___ them
8. ___ build	28. ___ knife	48. ___ they
9. ___ buy	29. ___ listen	49. ___ today
10. ___ careful	30. ___ lunch	50. ___ type
11. ___ clothes	31. ___ my	51. ___ us
12. ___ come	32. ___ never	52. ___ visit
13. ___ copy	33. ___ number	53. ___ weigh
14. ___ cry	34. ___ often	54. ___ white
15. ___ dinner	35. ___ our	55. ___ whole
16. ___ eight	36. ___ practice	56. ___ wild
17. ___ family	37. ___ price	57. ___ yellow
18. ___ guess	38. ___ rescue	58. ___ yesterday
19. ___ happy	39. ___ simple	59. ___ you
20. ___ heavy	40. ___ slowly	60. ___ your

25.4 Crossword Maze

25.5 Sort the E's

Write the words under the correct reason as your teacher dictates them.

The Vowel Says its Name Because of the E	English Words do not End in V	English Words do not End in U	The C says /s/ Because of the E

The G says /j/ Because of the E	Every Syllable Must have a Written Vowel	To Keep Singular Word from Ending in S	To Make the TH Voiced

Extra Practice

25.6 Silent E Reading List A

Read the words aloud. How many can you read in one minute?

bake	cave	article	flake	overdue	cursive	advice
have	dare	style	flame	hurtle	pine	alive
muffle	date	pave	frame	fine	pipe	twine
bale	temple	rage	glaze	struggle	ride	reduce
base	ease	rake	grade	simple	site	whine
battle	forgive	mumble	grape	whistle	size	code
cage	fade	rate	grave	griddle	tile	fumble
cake	fake	rave	plane	hide	time	coke
came	approve	safe	plate	settle	since	middle
change	true	hinge	mouse	hive	castle	cone
carve	fame	sale	quake	handle	wobble	cove
smuggle	game	same	scale	kite	wife	chive
cane	gate	save	stake	goose	rage	hole
give	stable	tame	forge	curve	wipe	hose
purge	gave	vase	state	life	glide	riddle
tricycle	kale	ice	trade	lime	brittle	lone
rescue	lake	wade	whale	mile	cable	improve
care	lame	nice	dribble	above	knife	mantle
spouse	truffle	wake	sphere	mine	bustle	value
race	lane	blame	bike	creative	stripe	axe
hurdle	late	candle	page	mite	horse	nose
case	pale	blaze	bite	pike	trike	due
truce	stage	drape	image	pile	vehicle	poke

25.6 Silent E Reading List B

Read the words aloud. How many can you read in one minute?

snore	duke	active	survive	pace	bye	wage
icicle	rattle	dance	chortle	ankle	bathe	wrinkle
waffle	fume	arrive	twelve	rice	teethe	large
example	huge	cave	kettle	vice	voice	image
spoke	mule	brace	avenue	triangle	wince	range
twice	pure	crave	blue	notice	promise	usage
miracle	rattle	fiddle	cause	noodle	bounce	dangle
space	rude	gave	cue	force	chance	five
stole	rule	glove	come	grace	choice	hike
eagle	tune	lace	couple	juice	fleece	babble
pursue	brute	groove	hue	mince	glance	single
store	shackle	bottle	crumple	ounce	voyage	cobble
mingle	fluke	humble	license	peace	palace	fable
cradle	byte	live	bundle	place	police	feeble
stove	twinkle	love	sue	pounce	prince	needle
whole	age	mauve	trickle	price	doodle	noble
wrote	hype	native	plunge	sauce	buckle	baffle
breathe	swerve	nerve	scarce	were	source	tremble
cube	bicycle	olive	shuffle	slice	grumble	circle
sample	apple	pave	lice	dimple	cripple	cycle
cute	mice	prove	bridle	spice	huge	dike
dude	clothe	rave	sponge	trace	urge	oracle

Extra Practice

25.7 Adding Suffixes

Write the new word.

1. _large + ly =_

2. _bake + er =_

3. _rescue + ed =_

4. _circle + ed =_

5. _noodle + s =_

6. _force + ful =_

7. _charge + able =_

8. _same + ness =_

9. _blame + less =_

10. _dance + er =_

11. _bounce + ing =_

12. _hike + er =_

13. _cage + s =_

14. _example + s =_

15. _ice + y =_

16. _vote + ed =_

17. _change + able =_

25.8 Adding Suffixes to Single Vowel Y Words

Write the new word.

1. *happy + ly =*
2. *baby + es =*
3. *fry + ing =*
4. *cry + ed =*
5. *body + es =*
6. *copy + es =*
7. *copy + ing =*
8. *cloudy + ness =*
9. *penny + less =*
10. *fly + er =*

Extra Practice

25.9 Adding Suffixes Chart

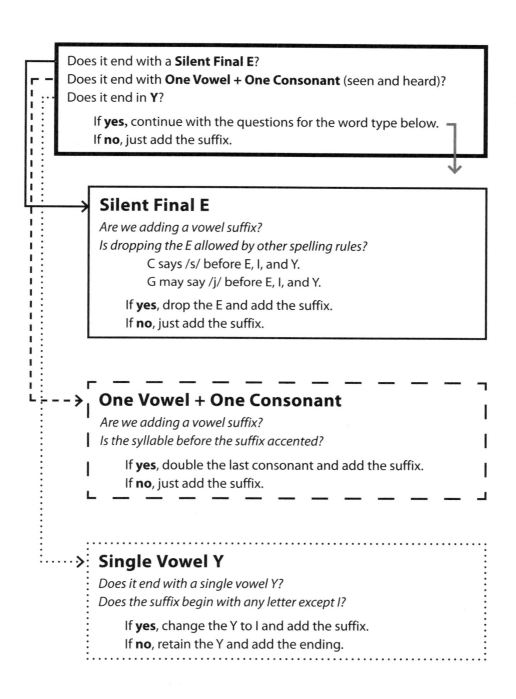

Does it end with a **Silent Final E**?
Does it end with **One Vowel + One Consonant** (seen and heard)?
Does it end in **Y**?

> If **yes**, continue with the questions for the word type below.
> If **no**, just add the suffix.

Silent Final E

Are we adding a vowel suffix?
Is dropping the E allowed by other spelling rules?
> C says /s/ before E, I, and Y.
> G may say /j/ before E, I, and Y.

If **yes**, drop the E and add the suffix.
If **no**, just add the suffix.

One Vowel + One Consonant

Are we adding a vowel suffix?
Is the syllable before the suffix accented?

If **yes**, double the last consonant and add the suffix.
If **no**, just add the suffix.

Single Vowel Y

Does it end with a single vowel Y?
Does the suffix begin with any letter except I?

If **yes**, change the Y to I and add the suffix.
If **no**, retain the Y and add the ending.

25.10 The Suffix -LY

Add the ending -LY to each word.

1. *happy* _____
2. *accident* _____
3. *day* _____
4. *large* _____
5. *light* _____
6. *mother* _____
7. *excellent* _____
8. *sharp* _____

25.11 ED Past Tense Ending

Write the words in the correct column as your teacher reads them.

/ĕd/	/d/	/t/
_____	_____	_____
_____	_____	_____
_____	_____	_____
_____	_____	_____
_____	_____	_____
_____	_____	_____
_____	_____	_____

25.12 Irregular Verbs

Match the present tense and past tense verbs.

~~bought~~	sold	saw	ate	heard
grew	made	took	fought	came
held	built	threw	sang	taught
knew	rode	caught	slept	thought
met	said	drew	found	

1. buy   *bought*

2. build

3. come

4. say

5. make

6. grow

7. ride

8. sell

9. see

10. teach

11. catch

12. draw

13. fight

14. hear

15. eat

16. hold

17. know

18. meet

19. take

20. sing

21. sleep

22. think

23. find

24. throw

25.13 Phonogram Quiz

Write the phonograms as your teacher dictates them.

1. _____	13. _____	25. _____	37. _____
2. _____	14. _____	26. _____	38. _____
3. _____	15. _____	27. _____	39. _____
4. _____	16. _____	28. _____	40. _____
5. _____	17. _____	29. _____	41. _____
6. _____	18. _____	30. _____	42. _____
7. _____	19. _____	31. _____	43. _____
8. _____	20. _____	32. _____	44. _____
9. _____	21. _____	33. _____	45. _____
10. _____	22. _____	34. _____	46. _____
11. _____	23. _____	35. _____	47. _____
12. _____	24. _____	36. _____	48. _____

49. _____

50. _____

51. _____

52. _____

53. _____

54. _____

55. _____

56. _____

57. _____

58. _____

59. _____

60. _____

61. _____

62. _____

63. _____

64. _____

65. _____

66. _____

Lesson 26

26.1 Writing the Phonogram

Write the new phonogram five times and say it aloud.

dge _____

26.2 Phonogram Practice

Write the phonograms as your teacher dictates them.

1. _____   6. _____   11. _____   16. _____

2. _____   7. _____   12. _____   17. _____

3. _____   8. _____   13. _____   18. _____

4. _____   9. _____   14. _____   19. _____

5. _____   10. _____   15. _____   20. _____

26.3 Phonogram Tic-Tac-Toe

dge	bu	gu
ei	ph	wor
wr	ui	ew

ew	ey	eigh
ei	ph	bu
kn	gu	dge

ir	ph	wor
tch	ei	bu
eigh	gu	dge

ow	wor	ph
gu	ei	wr
dge	bu	au

augh	eigh	igh
dge	ph	wr
kn	gn	ear

ei	dge	ey
ph	eigh	bu
gu	dge	ur

26.4 DGE

Read the words. Underline the DGE.

badge	drudge	judge	porridge
bridge	edge	ledge	ridge
budge	fidget	lodge	sledge
budget	fridge	midget	sludge
cartridge	fudge	nudge	smidgen
dodge	grudge	partridge	trudge
dredge	hedge	pledge	wedge

LIST 26

Spelling Words	Part of Speech	Plural Past Tense
1.		
2.		
3.		
4.		
5.		
6.		
7.		
8.		
9.		
10.		
11.		
12.		
13.		
14.		
15.		

26.5 Commands

Read the sentence. Underline the noun of direct address. Circle the comma.

Peter, tell me your brother's name.

Grace, show me the book.

Zander, close the door.

Read the sentence. Underline the noun of direct address. Circle the comma.

Open the trunk, Kayla.

Catch the frog, Austin.

Watch the ball, Jordan.

Read the sentence. Underline the noun of direct address. Circle the comma. Put a box around the word "please."

Peter, please bring me the newspaper.

Please talk quietly, girls.

Please, Rachel, throw this away.

26.6 Identifying Parts of Speech

Write the parts of speech over each word in the sentence as your teacher writes them on the board.

Read the book quietly.

Solve the six problems carefully.

Jacob, circle the first example.

Come here quickly, Samantha.

Lily, please carry the red bag.

Extra Practice

26.7 Statement or Command?

Read the sentence. Write **State.** on the line if it is a statement and **Com.** on the line if it is a command.

1. _____ Get the ball.

2. _____ Wash your hands.

3. _____ He solved an important case.

4. _____ The judge circled your name.

5. _____ Please carry the baby gently.

6. _____ He flew the airplane.

7. _____ Allison, find your coat.

8. _____ Read the example, Gavin.

9. _____ Three airplanes circled overhead.

10. _____ Sign your name.

26.8 Nouns of Direct Address

Add commas where needed in each of the sentences.

Joseph solve your math problems carefully.

Ryan listen closely.

Copy the words quickly Elizabeth.

Please Grandmother tell me a story.

Please feed the dog Morgan.

26.9 Editing

Each sentence includes three mistakes. Rewrite each one without the mistakes.

jack tell me your mothers name.

_____

_____

Alexandra copyed the storyes

_____

_____

please study the examples carefully justin.

_____

_____

26.10 Reading

Read the sentences aloud.

1. The people told wonderful stories.

2. The pilot flew the airplane north.

3. The judge learned each person's name.

4. Carry the large boxes over here.

5. The boy in the center is the tallest.

6. Please give me an example.

7. She said, "Bring me some water."

8. Please take the book over there.

9. Their class starts at noon.

10. Drink your water and eat your lunch.

26.11 Their and There

Fill in the correct word: their or there.

1. Help them find _____ keys.

2. Put your copy over _____.

3. This is _____ first time here.

4. I will put _____ watches on the table.

5. Take the children _____ for me.

26.12 Dictation

Listen to each sentence as your teacher reads it aloud. Repeat it back. Write it on the lines below.

1. _____

   _____

2. _____

   _____

3. _____

   _____

4. _____

   _____

5. _____

   _____

6. _____

   _____

26.13 Composition

Write five commands beginning with a person's name. You may use the following words for ideas, or create your own sentences.

Jacob	find	here
Lily	speak	paper
Emily	spell	word
Jack	carry	loudly
Wyatt	copy	softly
Alexis	come	carefully
Anna	watch	key
Molly	listen	baby

Wyatt, please watch the baby.

1. _____

_____

2. _____

_____

3. _____

_____

4. _____

_____

5. _____

_____

Lesson 27

27.1 The Phonogram IE

Read the words. Underline the IE.

field	yield	grieve	relieve
piece	brief	shield	shriek
fierce	chief	thief	priest
wield	grief	believe	

27.2 Writing the Phonogram

Write the new phonogram five times and say it aloud.

ie

27.3 Phonogram Practice

Write the phonograms as your teacher dictates them.

1. _____   6. _____   11. _____   16. _____

2. _____   7. _____   12. _____   17. _____

3. _____   8. _____   13. _____   18. _____

4. _____   9. _____   14. _____   19. _____

5. _____   10. _____   15. _____   20. _____

27.4 Phonogram Bingo

ei	ey	eigh	ay	ai
au	aw	augh	bu	gu
kn	gn	ur	ir	er
ear	ie	dge	ea	tch
oo	ou	ow	ph	wr

ai	ey	eigh	ay	gu
gn	ei	augh	au	wr
kn	ie	bu	ir	dge
ear	ea	ur	aw	tch
oo	ou	ow	er	ph

ie	gu	gn	ay	oo
ou	au	augh	ea	wr
kn	aw	bu	ir	eigh
ear	ow	ur	ei	tch
ph	er	dge	ey	ai

ou	tch	gu	gn	ai
kn	ea	augh	ir	ay
dge	ph	ie	aw	wr
ear	au	ei	ow	eigh
oo	er	ur	ey	bu

27.5 Spellings of Long /ē/

Write the spellings of long /ē/ below.

1. _____   3. _____   5. _____   7. _____

2. _____   4. _____   6. _____   8. _____

27.6 Spellings of the Long /ē/ Sound

Write the spellings of long /ē/ in the chart as your teacher writes them on the board.

End of the Syllable	Middle of the Syllable	End of a One-Syllable Word	End of a Multi-Syllable Word
_____	_____	_____	_____

27.7 Reading Words with the Long /ē/ Sound

Read the words below. Underline the phonogram that says the long /ē/ sound.

he	creak	chief	bee
fancy	protein	detail	jolly
meter	please	sweet	beetle
field	stream	hobby	she
me	remake	sweep	begin
barley	honey	hockey	team
clean	seize	screen	valley
piece	wreath	daily	brief

LIST 27

	Spelling Words	Part of Speech	Plural Past Tense
1.			
2.			
3.			
4.			
5.			
6.			
7.			
8.			
9.			
10.			
11.			
12.			
13.			
14.			
15.			

27.8 Be Verbs

Write the subject pronouns. Then write the present and past tense "Be" verbs.

Subject Pronouns	Present Tense Be Verbs	Past Tense Be Verbs
_____	_____	_____
_____	_____	_____
_____	_____	_____
_____	_____	_____
_____	_____	_____
_____	_____	_____
_____	_____	_____

27.9 Identifying Parts of Speech

Write the parts of speech as your teacher writes them on the board.

James is happy.

The house is yellow.

She is my niece.

They are bluebirds.

Extra Practice

27.10 "Be" Verbs

Complete the following sentences with the correct present tense form of the "Be Verb."

1. _She_ _____ _silent._
2. _They_ _____ _hungry._
3. _We_ _____ _late._
4. _I_ _____ _your niece._
5. _He_ _____ _your cousin._
6. _We_ _____ _a family._
7. _You_ _____ _a great basketball player._
8. _I_ _____ _cold._

27.11 Linking Verbs

Step 1: Underline the subject.

Step 2: Circle the linking verb.

Step 3: Divide the subject from the predicate.

Step 4: Underline the predicate adjective or noun that is describing the subject and draw an arrow back to the subject.

1. Ava is my cousin.

2. My uncles are hard workers.

3. Her nieces and nephews are wonderful.

4. My family is large.

5. They were good examples.

6. The fields were muddy.

7. She is an important person.

8. We are ready.

9. The problem is very difficult.

10. I am a student.

27.12 There or Their

Fill in the correct word: their or there.

1. _I found _____ coats._

2. _Put the books _____ ._

3. _The dogs ran in _____ own yard._

4. _Please take the boys _____ ._

5. _____ house is beautiful._

27.13 Editing

Each sentence includes three mistakes. Rewrite each one without the mistakes.

the three beautiful girls ar our nieces

_____

_____

I allways see my cousins their

_____

_____

Her uncl and aunt were hear

_____

_____

27.14 Contractions

Write the contractions.

1. *they + are =*

2. *we + are =*

3. *you + are =*

4. *she + is =*

5. *I + am =*

6. *it + is =*

7. *he + is =*

8. *that + is =*

27.15 Dictation

Listen to each sentence as your teacher reads it aloud. Repeat it back. Write it on the lines below.

1. _____

_____

2. _____

_____

3. _____

_____

4. _____

_____

5. _____

_____

6. _____

_____

27.16 Composition

Write 6 sentences with a subject pronoun, to be verb, noun or adjective.

I	am	happy
you	is	sad
he	are	tall
she	was	a student
it	were	my uncle
they		his cousin
we		her wife

I am happy.

1. _____

   _____

2. _____

   _____

3. _____

   _____

4. _____

   _____

5. _____

   _____

6. _____

   _____

Lesson 28

28.1 Phonogram Practice

Write the phonograms as your teacher dictates them.

1. _____	6. _____	11. _____	16. _____
2. _____	7. _____	12. _____	17. _____
3. _____	8. _____	13. _____	18. _____
4. _____	9. _____	14. _____	19. _____
5. _____	10. _____	15. _____	20. _____

28.2 Adding Suffixes Flow Chart

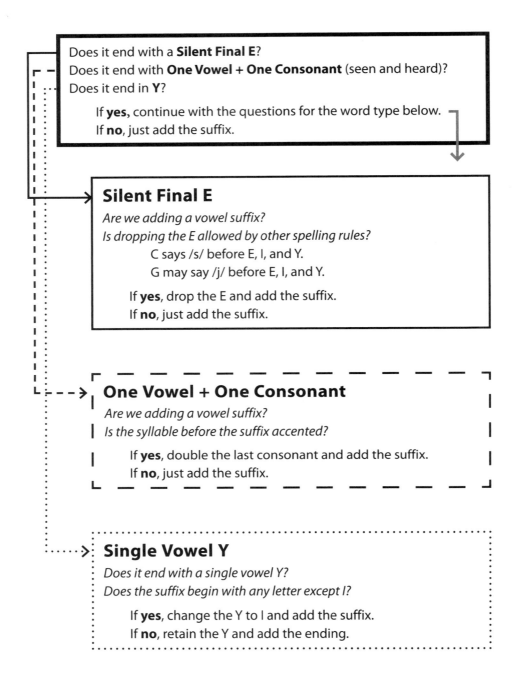

Does it end with a **Silent Final E**?
Does it end with **One Vowel + One Consonant** (seen and heard)?
Does it end in **Y**?

If **yes**, continue with the questions for the word type below.
If **no**, just add the suffix.

Silent Final E

Are we adding a vowel suffix?
Is dropping the E allowed by other spelling rules?
        C says /s/ before E, I, and Y.
        G may say /j/ before E, I, and Y.

If **yes**, drop the E and add the suffix.
If **no**, just add the suffix.

One Vowel + One Consonant

Are we adding a vowel suffix?
Is the syllable before the suffix accented?

If **yes**, double the last consonant and add the suffix.
If **no**, just add the suffix.

Single Vowel Y

Does it end with a single vowel Y?
Does the suffix begin with any letter except I?

If **yes**, change the Y to I and add the suffix.
If **no**, retain the Y and add the ending.

28.3 Adding Suffixes

Write the words as your teacher reads them.

1. _____

2. _____

3. _____

4. _____

5. _____

6. _____

7. _____

8. _____

28.4 Phonograms that say /ow/

Write the phonograms which say /ow/.

1. _____   2. _____   3. _____

28.5 Words Ending with OW

Read the words aloud. Underline the /ow/.

bow	cow	plow	vow
brow	how	prow	wow
chow	now	sow	

28.6 Words Spelled with OW in the Middle of the Syllable

Read the words aloud. Underline the OW.

down	drown	vowel	glower
brown	gown	power	browse
town	growl	tower	
clown	yowl	powder	
crown	fowl	shower	

28.7 Words Spelled with OU in the Middle of the Syllable

Read the words aloud. Underline the /ow/.

couch	compound	devout	dour
vouch	account	scout	sour
cloud	noun	route	flour
loud	foul	snout	house
proud	doubt	stout	blouse
shroud	mount	trout	grouse
bound	about	mouth	joust
hound	out	scour	mouse
found	spout	devour	ounce

LIST 28

Spelling Words	Part of Speech	Plural Past Tense
1.		
2.		
3.		
4.		
5.		
6.		
7.		
8.		
9.		
10.		
11.		
12.		
13.		
14.		
15.		

28.8 Numbers

Write the numbers as your teacher reads them aloud.

1. _____

2. _____

3. _____

4. _____

5. _____

6. _____

7. _____

8. _____

9. _____

28.9 Number Reference Chart

Write the numbers.

1 _____	18 _____
2 _____	19 _____
3 _____	20 _____
4 _____	30 _____
5 _____	40 _____
6 _____	50 _____
7 _____	60 _____
8 _____	70 _____
9 _____	80 _____
10 _____	90 _____
11 _____	100 _____
12 _____	1000 _____
13 _____	1/2 _____
14 _____	1/3 _____
15 _____	1/4 _____
16 _____	1/5 _____
17 _____	1/6 _____

28.10 Numbers

Rewrite each sentence using the correct form of the number.

1. *School starts at 8:00 A.M.*

2. *There are 28 students.*

3. *We biked 100 miles.*

4. *She left at 3:46 P.M.*

5. *3/4 of the pie is left.*

28.11 Identifying Parts of Speech

Write the parts of speech as your teacher writes them on the board.

Her nephews are twins.

Four fields are almost dry.

The judge is important.

She is always alone.

28.12 Ordinal Numbers

Read each of the ordinal numbers. Highlight words as your teacher directs you.

first	eighteenth	thirty-fifth
second	nineteenth	thirty-sixth
third	twentieth	thirty-seventh
fourth	twenty-first	thirty-eighth
fifth	twenty-second	thirty-ninth
sixth	twenty-third	fortieth
seventh	twenty-fourth	forty-first
eighth	twenty-fifth	forty-second
ninth	twenty-sixth	forty-third
tenth	twenty-seventh	forty-fourth
eleventh	twenty-eighth	forty-fifth
twelfth	twenty-ninth	forty-sixth
thirteenth	thirtieth	forty-seventh
fourteenth	thirty-first	forty-eighth
fifteenth	thirty-second	forty-ninth
sixteenth	thirty-third	fiftieth
seventeenth	thirty-fourth	

28.13 Ordinal Numbers

Write the ordinal numbers.

1st _____

2nd _____

3rd _____

4th _____

5th _____

6th _____

7th _____

8th _____

9th _____

10th _____

11th _____

12th _____

13th _____

14th _____

15th _____

16th _____

17th _____

18th _____

19th _____

20th _____

30th _____

40th _____

50th _____

60th _____

70th _____

80th _____

90th _____

100th _____

1000th _____

28.14 Ordinal Numbers in Sentences

Rewrite each sentence using the correct form of the ordinal number.

1. *She finished the race 1st.*

2. *He was 5th in line.*

3. *The black car finished 20th.*

4. *She is in 9th place.*

5. *That was the 12th time it happened.*

28.15 Checks

Write checks using today's date and the information below:

Quality Mattress Company
$341.69

```
_____ Date

Pay to the

order of _____  [ $              ]

_____Dollars


_____
```

The Great Toy Shop
$44.32

```
_____ Date

Pay to the

order of _____  [ $              ]

_____Dollars


_____
```

Pete's Pizza
$12.90

_____ Date

Pay to the

order of _____ $ [   ]

_____Dollars

_____

The Pumpkin Patch
$8.21

_____ Date

Pay to the

order of _____ $ [   ]

_____Dollars

_____

28.16 Dictation

Listen to each sentence as your teacher reads it aloud. Repeat it back. Write it on the lines below.

1. _____

   _____

2. _____

   _____

3. _____

   _____

4. _____

   _____

5. _____

   _____

6. _____

   _____

28.17 Composition

Write a sentence which includes a list of six items and their quantities that you bought at the store. Use at least three hyphenated numbers.

_____

_____

_____

_____

_____

_____

_____

_____

_____

_____

Lesson 29

29.1 Writing the Phonograms

Write the new phonograms five times each and say them aloud.

ti _____

si _____

ci _____

29.2 Phonogram Practice

Write the phonograms as your teacher dictates them.

1. _____   6. _____   11. _____   16. _____

2. _____   7. _____   12. _____   17. _____

3. _____   8. _____   13. _____   18. _____

4. _____   9. _____   14. _____   19. _____

5. _____   10. _____   15. _____   20. _____

29.3 Latin Spellings of /sh/

Read the words. Underline the phonograms that say /sh/.

action	discussion	shining	share
ship	partial	finish	fishing
expression	publish	social	famish
physician	accomplish	tension	confession

29.4 The Spellings of /sh/

Write the words in the column based upon the spelling of /sh/.

SH	TI, CI, SI
_____	_____
_____	_____
_____	_____
_____	_____
_____	_____
_____	_____
_____	_____

29.5 Latin Roots

Match the root to the derivative. Underline the letter that determined which Latin spelling of /sh/ would be used in the derivative.

~~action~~   motivation   expression   tension   discussion
adoption   clinician   intimidation   Egyptian   musician
spacial   politician   creation   vibration   racial

act	*action*
politic	
race	
express	
motivate	
space	
music	
discuss	
create	
intimidate	
clinic	
adopt	
tense	
Egypt	
vibrate	

LIST 29

Spelling Words	Part of Speech	Plural Past Tense
1.		
2.		
3.		
4.		
5.		
6.		
7.		
8.		
9.		
10.		
11.		
12.		
13.		
14.		
15.		

29.6 Contractions

Write the contractions.

1. they + are = _____

2. we + are = _____

3. you + are = _____

4. I + am = _____

5. it + is = _____

6. he + is = _____

7. she + is = _____

8. that + is = _____

29.7 Interjections

Read the sentences aloud. Write I over the interjection. Circle the punctuation after each interjection. What do you notice?

1. Ahh, that feels good.

2. Help! He stole my purse!

3. Ouch! You hit me!

4. Hey! Come back here!

5. Wow! I won!

6. Oh, that's it.

7. Eh, that looks great.

8. Hmm, I think this is the right one.

9. Uh-oh, you spilled it.

10. Yes! You did it!

29.8 Identifying Parts of Speech

Write the parts of speech as your teacher writes them on the board.

Yikes! That is a strange expression!

Good job! Those are the right answers.

The officials quietly gave me the directions.

My two uncles quickly solved the difficult problem.

29.9 Their and There

Fill in the correct word: their or there.

1. *I brought _____ warm clothes.*
2. *The officials will stand _____.*
3. *That is _____ house.*
4. *They live _____.*
5. *_____ is no place like home.*
6. *_____ dog ran away last week.*

29.10 Homophones

Circle the correct spelling.

1. What is their/there last name?

2. Can you hear/here the music clearly?

3. What time will you be their/there?

4. They brought their/there swimsuits.

5. Will you bring the puppy over hear/here?

Extra Practice

29.11 Editing

Each sentence includes three mistakes. Rewrite each one without the mistakes.

The officials acshons were strang.

_____

_____

one niece two cousins five uncles, and four aunts visited us.

_____

_____

this is the highest brij

_____

_____

29.12 Vocabulary Development

Add the endings to each word.

1. workman + ship = _____

2. leader + ship = _____

3. owner + ship = _____

4. relation + ship = _____

5. office + ial = _____

6. invent + ion = _____

7. express + ion = _____

8. act + ion = _____

9. direct + ion = _____

29.13 Numbers

Rewrite each sentence using the correct form of the number.

1. *Those are 3 wonderful inventions.*

2. *There are 32 officials.*

3. *The building has 41 offices.*

4. *The party started at 4:00.*

5. *The birthday cake is 1/2 gone.*

29.14 Dictation

Listen to each sentence as your teacher reads it aloud. Repeat it back. Write it on the lines below.

1. _____

_____

2. _____

_____

3. _____

_____

4. _____

_____

5. _____

_____

6. _____

_____

29.15 Composition

Complete each sentence.

1. *They are* _____

2. *My twenty-seven cousins* _____

3. *The important judge* _____

4. *Two airplanes* _____

Lesson 30

30.1 Assessment

Listen to each phrase as your teacher dictates. Repeat it back. Write it on the lines below.

1. _____

_____

2. _____

_____

3. _____

_____

4. _____

_____

5. _____

_____

6. _____

_____

7. _____

_____

8. _____

_____

9. _____

_____

10. _____

_____

30.2 Reading

Read the sentences.

1. The teacher wrote the directions and examples on the board.

2. I feel alone.

3. He carried five watches and two phones.

4. Center the photograph on the wall.

5. Circle each example.

6. The corn in the large field is ripe.

7. The pilots flew the airplanes in formation.

8. My uncle gave his son one hundred dollars.

9. The husband and wife waited.

10. The lone bird flew over the lake.

11. Our nieces and nephews are beautiful people.

12. I need the right tools.

13. We will solve the problem.

14. Forty people signed up for class.

15. We were there twice this year.

16. His wife turned twenty-nine yesterday.

17. My cousins are twins.

30.3 Words to practice

Mark the spelling words which need more practice.

1. ____ actions	21. ____ forty	41. ____ please
2. ____ airplane	22. ____ four	42. ____ ready
3. ____ almost	23. ____ here	43. ____ rise
4. ____ alone	24. ____ high	44. ____ solve
5. ____ always	25. ____ hundred	45. ____ strange
6. ____ are	26. ____ husband	46. ____ that
7. ____ be	27. ____ important	47. ____ there
8. ____ bridge	28. ____ invention	48. ____ these
9. ____ carry	29. ____ is	49. ____ this
10. ____ center	30. ____ judge	50. ____ those
11. ____ circle	31. ____ lone	51. ____ thousand
12. ____ cousin	32. ____ nephew	52. ____ twelve
13. ____ directions	33. ____ niece	53. ____ twenty
14. ____ each	34. ____ office	54. ____ twice
15. ____ example	35. ____ official	55. ____ twin
16. ____ expression	36. ____ one	56. ____ two
17. ____ field	37. ____ only	57. ____ uncle
18. ____ fifty	38. ____ party	58. ____ was
19. ____ five	39. ____ people	59. ____ were
20. ____ fly	40. ____ person	60. ____ wife

30.4 The Spellings of /sh/

Write the words in the column based upon the spelling of /sh/. (The columns continue on the next page.)

SH	TI
_____	_____
_____	_____
_____	_____
_____	_____
_____	_____
_____	_____

30.4 The Spellings of /sh/ Continued

SI	CI

Extra Practice

30.5 Adding Suffixes Flow Chart

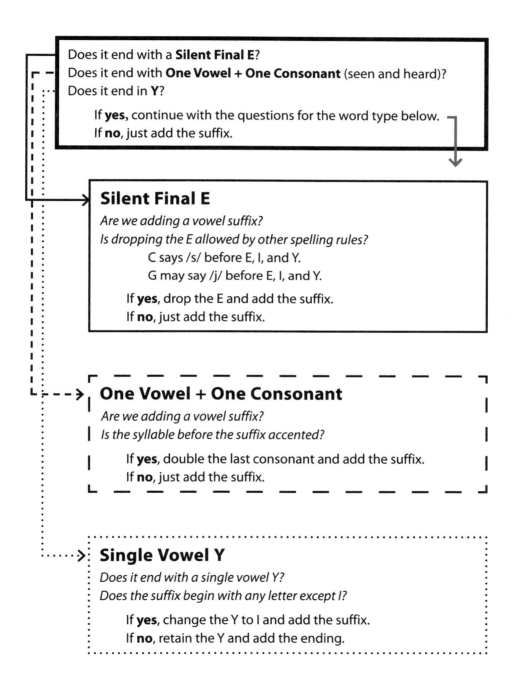

Does it end with a **Silent Final E**?
Does it end with **One Vowel + One Consonant** (seen and heard)?
Does it end in **Y**?

If **yes,** continue with the questions for the word type below.
If **no,** just add the suffix.

Silent Final E

Are we adding a vowel suffix?
Is dropping the E allowed by other spelling rules?
        C says /s/ before E, I, and Y.
        G may say /j/ before E, I, and Y.

If **yes,** drop the E and add the suffix.
If **no,** just add the suffix.

One Vowel + One Consonant

Are we adding a vowel suffix?
Is the syllable before the suffix accented?

If **yes,** double the last consonant and add the suffix.
If **no,** just add the suffix.

Single Vowel Y

Does it end with a single vowel Y?
Does the suffix begin with any letter except I?

If **yes,** change the Y to I and add the suffix.
If **no,** retain the Y and add the ending.

30.6 Adding Suffixes

Write the words as your teacher reads them.

1. _____

2. _____

3. _____

4. _____

5. _____

6. _____

7. _____

8. _____

9. _____

10. _____

11. _____

12. _____

13. _____

14. _____

15. _____

16. _____

30.7 Homophones

Circle the correct form of each homophone.

1. I hear/here my brother talking.

2. Its/It's late.

3. Their/There/They're plane arrived late.

4. Your/You're package arrived.

5. Their/There/They're planning a birthday party for him.

6. Your/You're a good judge.

7. They are hear/here.

8. The cat licked its/it's paws.

9. Take the dish over their/there/they're.

30.8 Numbers

Write the numbers.

53 _____

42 _____

13 _____

12 _____

22 _____

98 _____

30.9 Checks

Fill out the checks, writing the numbers correctly.

Sam's Sandwiches
$22.00

```
┌──────────────────────────────────────────────────────────┐
│                                                            │
│                          _____  Date    │
│                                                            │
│  Pay to the                                                │
│                                          ┌──────────────┐  │
│  order of _____  │ $            │  │
│                                          └──────────────┘  │
│  _____Dollars      │
│                                                            │
│                          _____      │
└──────────────────────────────────────────────────────────┘
```

The Ski Hut
$81.99

```
┌──────────────────────────────────────────────────────────┐
│                                                            │
│                          _____  Date    │
│                                                            │
│  Pay to the                                                │
│                                          ┌──────────────┐  │
│  order of _____  │ $            │  │
│                                          └──────────────┘  │
│  _____Dollars      │
│                                                            │
│                          _____      │
└──────────────────────────────────────────────────────────┘
```

30.10 Contractions

Write the contractions.

1. _they + are = _____

2. _we + are = _____

3. _you + are = _____

4. _she + is = _____

5. _I + am = _____

6. _it + is = _____

7. _he + is = _____

8. _that + is = _____

30.11 Contractions

Write the words that form the contraction.

1. *that's* = _____

2. *they're* = _____

3. *he's* = _____

4. *we're* = _____

5. *it's* = _____

6. *she's* = _____

7. *I'm* = _____

8. *you're* = _____

30.12 Phonogram Quiz

Write the phonograms as your teacher dictates them.

1. _____	13. _____	25. _____	37. _____
2. _____	14. _____	26. _____	38. _____
3. _____	15. _____	27. _____	39. _____
4. _____	16. _____	28. _____	40. _____
5. _____	17. _____	29. _____	41. _____
6. _____	18. _____	30. _____	42. _____
7. _____	19. _____	31. _____	43. _____
8. _____	20. _____	32. _____	44. _____
9. _____	21. _____	33. _____	45. _____
10. _____	22. _____	34. _____	46. _____
11. _____	23. _____	35. _____	47. _____
12. _____	24. _____	36. _____	48. _____

49._____

50._____

51._____

52._____

53._____

54._____

55._____

56._____

57._____

58._____

59._____

60._____

61._____

62._____

63._____

64._____

65._____

66._____

67._____

68._____

69._____

30.13 Speed Bingo

Dictate phonograms for review. Provide students with something to cover each square. Call out the phonograms for the students to cover, one phonogram every 2-5 seconds. Students must hunt quickly for the phonogram. The first person with 5 in-a-row wins.

Lesson 31

31

31.1 The CEI Phonogram

Read the words. Underline the CEI.

ceiling   receipt   deceit   conceive

receive   deceive   conceit   perceive

31.2 Writing the Phonograms

Write the new phonogram five times and say it aloud.

cei _____

31.3 Phonogram Practice

Write the phonograms as your teacher dictates them.

1. _____   6. _____   11. _____   16. _____

2. _____   7. _____   12. _____   17. _____

3. _____   8. _____   13. _____   18. _____

4. _____   9. _____   14. _____   19. _____

5. _____   10. _____   15. _____   20. _____

31.4 Accent

Mark the accent in each word with an accent mark. See the first word for an example.

rock' et

la zy

a bout

lum ber

be tween

lit tle

chick en

mar ble

liz ard

po lice

to day

af ter noon

un der stand

for get ful

tel e phone

cam er a

mu si cal

LIST 31

Spelling Words	Part of Speech	Plural Past Tense
1.		
2.		
3.		
4.		
5.		
6.		
7.		
8.		
9.		
10.		
11.		
12.		
13.		
14.		
15.		

31.5 Prepositions

List the prepositions of location that work in the following sentence.

The cat is _____ the box(es).

1. _____   7. _____   13. _____

2. _____   8. _____   14. _____

3. _____   9. _____   15. _____

4. _____   10. _____   16. _____

5. _____   11. _____   17. _____

6. _____   12. _____

31.6 Identifying Parts of Speech

Label the parts of speech as your teacher labels them on the board.

The new airplane is on the runway.

The storm clouds are over the mountains.

She looked under the window.

I hear a strange noise in the ceiling.

31.7 Prepositional Phrases

Write a P over the preposition and put parentheses around the prepositional phrase. Illustrate each sentence.

The dog is on the doghouse.	The dog is in the doghouse.
The dog is by the doghouse.	The dog is over the doghouse.
The dog is between the doghouses.	The dog is under the doghouse.
The dog is above the doghouse.	The dog is below the doghouse.

31.8 Dictation

Listen to each sentence as your teacher reads it aloud. Repeat it back. Write it on the lines below.

1. _____

_____

2. _____

_____

3. _____

_____

4. _____

_____

5. _____

_____

6. _____

_____

31.9 Composition

Complete the sentences with a prepositional phrase. Use one of the following prepositions: by, over, between, under, above, at, below, near.

1. *Two children played*

2. *The official sat*

3. *His twelve uncles live*

4. *My cell phone is*

5. *The judge looked*

6. *The airplane flew*

31.10 Vocabulary Development

Write the new words formed by adding the prefix. Use each new word in a sentence out loud.

1. over + ride =
2. under + sold =
3. over + charge =
4. over + throw =
5. under + hand =
6. over + value =
7. over + reach =

Challenge

31.11 CEI Words

Use the correct form of each word in the sentences below.

ceiling	deceit	conceit	receipt
deceive	conceive	receive	perceive

1. *Before I return the game, I must find my* _____ .

2. *My mother always* _____ *when I do not tell the truth.*

3. *Do not* _____ *the teacher. You must tell her the truth.*

4. *Look! A large spider is crawling across the* _____ .

5. _____ *is the wrong way to handle a mistake. Always tell the truth.*

6. _The author_ _____ _the idea_
for this book in 2001. _____

7. _The_ _____ _boy thinks_
he is the best. _____

8. _Aunt Jane_ _____ _a_
package. _____

Lesson 32

32.1 Phonogram Practice

Write the phonograms as your teacher dictates them.

1. _____	6. _____	11. _____	16. _____
2. _____	7. _____	12. _____	17. _____
3. _____	8. _____	13. _____	18. _____
4. _____	9. _____	14. _____	19. _____
5. _____	10. _____	15. _____	20. _____

32.2 Double Consonants

Read the words. Mark the vowel in the first syllable long or short.

di ner	din ner	bab ble	ba by
pa per	hap py	fun nel	fu ner al

32.3 Double Consonants

Read the words. Divide the syllables.

forget   whisper   enjoy

32.4 Practice Words

Write the words as your teacher dictates them.

1. _____   5. _____

2. _____   6. _____

3. _____   7. _____

4. _____   8. _____

32.5 Words Ending in One Vowel and One Consonant

Read the words.

run	slip	ship	cup
bag	win	drop	
stop	swim	plan	

32.6 Adding Suffixes

Add the suffixes to each of the words.

	Double the Last Consonant	Do not Double the Last Consonant
1. bag -ful -ing	*bagging*	*bagful*
2. ship -ing -ment		
3. mad -en -ly		
4. pup -s -y		
5. snug -est -ly		
6. sad -ly -en		
7. big -er -ness		
8. hot -ly -er		
9. bug -y -s		
10. wet -ness -er		

32.7 Reading Words

Read the words. Circle the words as your teacher reads them.

hopping	cutter	robbed	pinning
hoping	cuter	robed	pining

32.8 Pairs of Words

Read the words. Circle the words as your teacher reads them.

1. robbed   robed

2. hopping   hoping

3. pining   pinning

4. cuter   cutter

32.9 Writing Words

Write the words as your teacher dictates them.

1. _____

2. _____

3. _____

4. _____

5. _____

6. _____

Extra Practice

32.10 Accent

Mark the accent in each word.

in to   a mount

de sign   des pite

ser vice   a lone

a ble   ac cept

in stead   re view

suc cess   o pen

ma jor   un less

a ward

LIST 32

	Spelling Words	Part of Speech	Plural Past Tense
1.			
2.			
3.			
4.			
5.			
6.			
7.			
8.			
9.			
10.			
11.			
12.			
13.			
14.			
15.			

32.11 Prepositions

Create sentences aloud using the action verbs and prepositions listed below.

Action verbs		Prepositions	
tiptoe	drive	past	to
march	jump	onto	up
stamp	skate	into	around
run	talk	upon	beside
kneel	stomp	down	across
throw	climb	toward	off
walk	swim	out	through
bike		of	

32.12 Identifying Parts of Speech

Write the parts of speech for each sentence as your teacher writes them on the board.

The happy winners ran around their school.

My cousins raced across the yard, down the street, and to the hospital.

The brown squirrel suddenly ran up the tree.

32.13 Practicing Prepositions

Write a P over the preposition and put parentheses around the prepositional phrase. Illustrate each sentence.

We rode a bus to school.	The dog walked around the tree.
Her books are beside the table.	He walked toward the lake.
The glass fell off the counter.	A lizard climbed out of its cage.
A child crawled through the tunnel.	She drew a line across the paper.

32.14 Paragraphs

Read the paragraphs. Draw a line under the indent. Circle the capital letters and the end marks.

Emma and I raced through the house, down the street, across the park, around the corner, and to our grandmother's house. We knocked on her door and waited. Our sweet grandmother opened the door and invited us inside. Grandma made us lunch. I sat beside Emma. Grandma sat across from me. Grandma told us stories. We had a wonderful time.

A young girl ran the fastest time. She was the winner at the school race. After the race, she stood on a platform and received a gold medal. As she waved at the people, a photographer took her picture for the newspaper. Her teacher gave her one yellow flower. She felt happy.

My aunt and uncle hiked in the mountains. They walked through thick forests and saw beautiful trees. One night they camped by a river. A bear tried to eat their food. Thankfully it was tied high up in a tree. They enjoyed their trip.

Two people walked toward the house. They stopped. They looked around the yard. Slowly they opened the door and slipped inside. Then they shouted, "Surprise! Happy Birthday!"

32.15 Dictation

Listen to each sentence as your teacher reads it aloud. Repeat it back. Write it on the lines below.

_____

_____

_____

_____

_____

_____

_____

_____

_____

_____

_____

_____

32.16 Composition

Read the simple sentence. Add the part of speech directed by each step and rewrite the sentence.

The winner stopped.

Adjective:

Three winners stopped.

Adverb:

_____

Prepositional Phrase:

_____

_____

Adjective:

_____

_____

_____

Prepositional Phrase:

_____

_____

_____

32.17 Vocabulary Development

How many words can you find that include the word "down?"

_____

_____

_____

_____

_____

_____

_____

_____

_____

_____

_____

_____

_____

_____

_____

_____

Lesson 33

33.1 Phonogram Practice

Write the phonograms as your teacher dictates them.

1. _____   6. _____   11. _____   16. _____

2. _____   7. _____   12. _____   17. _____

3. _____   8. _____   13. _____   18. _____

4. _____   9. _____   14. _____   19. _____

5. _____   10. _____   15. _____   20. _____

33.2 Adding Suffixes

Add the suffixes to each of the words. Write each word in the correct column. Divide it into syllables and write an accent mark on the accented syllable.

	Double the last consonant	Do not double the last consonant
1. limit -ing		lim' it ing
2. control -ed	con trol' led	
3. forget -ful		
4. equip -ing		
5. medal -ist		
6. begin -er		
7. forget -able		
8. forget -ing		
9. prefer -ed		
10. prefer -ence		

33.3 Accent

Mark the accented syllable in each of the words.

prob lem   per son

re turn   of fice

be hind   her self

lev el   fath er

a go   stud y

in deed   ac count

bod y

LIST 33

Spelling Words	Part of Speech	Plural Past Tense
1.		
2.		
3.		
4.		
5.		
6.		
7.		
8.		
9.		
10.		
11.		
12.		
13.		
14.		
15.		

33.4 Identifying Parts of Speech

Label the parts of speech in your workbook as I write them on the board.

She is brushing her teeth.

Dad is fixing the car in our driveway.

We are studying math in school.

33.5 Helping Verbs

Use the correct helping verb in each sentence.

am   is   are

1. *She   beginning tennis lessons next week.*

2. *We   receiving the letters.*

3. *He   taking the dog for a walk.*

4. *I   stopping.*

5. *They   racing.*

33.6 Present Continuous Story

Read the story. What do you notice about this story?

I am reading a book and waiting. The shop is fixing my car. The workers are taking a long time. Their team is going to lunch. I am still waiting.

33.7 Composition

Write a short story. It must have at least five sentences. It must be told in present continuous tense, as if the story is happening right now.

_____

_____

_____

_____

_____

_____

_____

_____

_____

_____

_____

_____

33.8 Vocabulary Development

Add the suffixes to form new words. Be careful to listen for the accent.

1. begin + er =
2. begin + ing =
3. prefer + able =
4. fix + ed =
5. forget + ing =
6. forget + able =
7. present + s =
8. vacation + ing =
9. receive + ed =
10. team + ing =

33.9 Dictation

Listen to each sentence as your teacher reads it aloud. Repeat it back. Write it on the lines below in paragraph form.

_____

_____

_____

_____

_____

_____

_____

_____

_____

_____

_____

Lesson 34

34.1 Phonogram Practice

Write the phonograms as your teacher dictates them.

1. _____	6. _____	11. _____	16. _____
2. _____	7. _____	12. _____	17. _____
3. _____	8. _____	13. _____	18. _____
4. _____	9. _____	14. _____	19. _____
5. _____	10. _____	15. _____	20. _____

34.2 Words with a Silent L

Read the words below that have a silent L.

walk	would	half
talk	should	halve
chalk	calf	salmon
could	calve	Lincoln

34.3 Words with a Silent L

Write the words with a silent L below. Underline the silent L with a different color.

1. _____

2. _____

3. _____

4. _____

5. _____

6. _____

7. _____

8. _____

9. _____

10. _____

11. _____

12. _____

34.4 Adding a Suffix to Any Word

Does it end with a **Silent Final E**?
Does it end with **One Vowel + One Consonant** (seen and heard)?
Does it end in **Y**?

> If **yes**, continue with the questions for the word type below.
> If **no**, just add the suffix.

Silent Final E

Are we adding a vowel suffix?
Is dropping the E allowed by other spelling rules?
> C says /s/ before E, I, and Y.
> G may say /j/ before E, I, and Y.

> If **yes**, drop the E and add the suffix.
> If **no**, just add the suffix.

One Vowel + One Consonant

Are we adding a vowel suffix?
Is the syllable before the suffix accented?

> If **yes**, double the last consonant and add the suffix.
> If **no**, just add the suffix.

Single Vowel Y

Does it end with a single vowel Y?
Does the suffix begin with any letter except I?

> If **yes**, change the Y to I and add the suffix.
> If **no**, retain the Y and add the ending.

34.5 Adding Suffixes

Add the suffixes to form new words.

1. receive + ed = _____

2. fix + ing = _____

3. noise + y = _____

4. vacation + ed = _____

5. forget + ful = _____

6. win + er = _____

7. surprise + ing = _____

8. sudden + ly = _____

9. look + ed = _____

10. unforget + able = _____

11. airplane + s = _____

12. carry + ed = _____

13. party + es = _____

14. strange + er = _____

15. please + ing = _____

LIST 34

	Spelling Words	Part of Speech	Plural Past Tense
1.			
2.			
3.			
4.			
5.			
6.			
7.			
8.			
9.			
10.			
11.			
12.			
13.			
14.			
15.			

34.6 Helping Verb List

Write the helping verbs as your teacher dictates them.

_____	_____	_____
_____	_____	_____
_____	_____	_____
_____		
_____		
_____		
_____		

_____	_____	_____
_____	_____	_____
_____	_____	_____

34.7 Helping Verbs

Form sentences aloud using a helping verb and action verb.

am	add
is	agree
are	control
was	decide
were	begin
be	prefer
being	receive
been	fix
have	forget
has	present
had	stop
do	win
does	surprise
did	look
may	store
might	answer
must	attend
should	celebrate
could	center
would	change
can	circle
will	copy
shall	express

34.8 Irregular Verbs

Choose the correct verb to complete the sentence. Write it in the blank: am, is, are, have, has, do, does, go, goes

1. _I_ _____ going home.

2. _She_ _____ a beautiful name.

3. _They_ _____ my cousins.

4. _Ella_ _____ not know the answer.

5. _I_ _____ to school with them.

6. _He_ _____ an enormous black dog.

7. _She_ _____ to practice at ten o'clock today.

8. _They_ _____ not want to come with us.

9. _We_ _____ a great game we can play.

10. _It_ _____ cold outside.

34.9 Future Tense

Change each of the sentences to future tense.

1. *I made the decision.*

2. *My mother works at the school.*

3. *The official forgot the answer.*

4. *My sister takes ice skating lessons.*

5. *Our team began practice.*

34.10 Identifying Parts of Speech

Label the parts of speech in your workbook as I write them on the board.

The judge will decide the case on Monday.

We will go on vacation soon.

The noises across the hall will stop tomorrow.

34.11 Contractions

Write the contractions formed with "will."

I + will = _____

you + will = _____

he + will = _____

she + will = _____

it + will = _____

we + will = _____

they + will = _____

34.12 Contractions

Write the contractions formed with "would."

I + would = _____

you + would = _____

he + would = _____

she + would = _____

it + would = _____

we + would = _____

they + would = _____

34.13 Contractions

Write the contractions formed with "have."

I + have = _____

you + have = _____

she + has = _____

he + has = _____

it + has = _____

we + have = _____

they + have = _____

34.14 Contractions

Cut out the cards on the following page. Find the matching pairs.

I have	**he'd**
you would	**we'll**
they have	**I've**
I will	**I'm**
we are	**it'd**
he would	**she'll**
we will	**you'd**
I am	**we're**
it would	**they've**
she will	**they're**
they are	**I'll**

34.15 Dictation

Listen to each sentence as your teacher reads it aloud. Repeat it back. Write it on the lines below in paragraph form.

_____

_____

_____

_____

_____

_____

_____

_____

_____

_____

_____

_____

_____

_____

34.16 Composition

Using each of the sentence starters, write the rest of the sentence.

Tomorrow I will

He should have

They've

You could

She might

Lesson 35

35

35.1 Assessment

Listen to each phrase as your teacher dictates. Repeat it back. Write it on the lines below.

1. _____

_____

2. _____

_____

3. _____

_____

4. _____

_____

5. _____

_____

6. _____

_____

7. _____

_____

8. _____

_____

9. _____

_____

10. _____

_____

35.2 Reading

Read the sentences.

1. His mother said, "The decision was his alone."

2. The water poured over the tub, down the stairs, around the corner, and out the door.

3. He prefers fixing his own car.

4. His apartment is above the store.

5. I do not have any toothpaste left.

6. She has been to that school.

7. The land in Holland is below sea level.

8. We live between two white houses.

9. There are many sharp pieces of glass by the swing.

10. She does not understand the answer.

11. The students have done wonderful work this year.

12. You might enjoy the books on the shelves.

13. He said the program would start at eight o'clock.

35.3 Words to Practice

Mark the spelling words which need more practice.

1.	_____ above	22.	_____ forgetful	43.	_____ several
2.	_____ across	23.	_____ from	44.	_____ should
3.	_____ any	24.	_____ have	45.	_____ stopped
4.	_____ around	25.	_____ hospital	46.	_____ store
5.	_____ been	26.	_____ look	47.	_____ suddenly
6.	_____ beginner	27.	_____ many	48.	_____ surprise
7.	_____ below	28.	_____ may	49.	_____ team
8.	_____ beside	29.	_____ medicine	50.	_____ through
9.	_____ between	30.	_____ might	51.	_____ to
10.	_____ by	31.	_____ mountain	52.	_____ tomorrow
11.	_____ ceiling	32.	_____ near	53.	_____ took
12.	_____ controlling	33.	_____ noise	54.	_____ toward
13.	_____ could	34.	_____ of	55.	_____ under
14.	_____ decide	35.	_____ off	56.	_____ vacation
15.	_____ decision	36.	_____ out	57.	_____ will
16.	_____ do	37.	_____ over	58.	_____ window
17.	_____ does	38.	_____ prefer	59.	_____ winner
18.	_____ done	39.	_____ present	60.	_____ would
19.	_____ down	40.	_____ race		
20.	_____ fix	41.	_____ receive		
21.	_____ for	42.	_____ sea		

35.4 Word Search

<table>
<tr><td></td><td></td><td></td><td></td><td></td><td></td><td></td><td></td><td></td><td></td></tr>
<tr><td></td><td></td><td></td><td></td><td></td><td></td><td></td><td></td><td></td><td></td></tr>
<tr><td></td><td></td><td></td><td></td><td></td><td></td><td></td><td></td><td></td><td></td></tr>
<tr><td></td><td></td><td></td><td></td><td></td><td></td><td></td><td></td><td></td><td></td></tr>
<tr><td></td><td></td><td></td><td></td><td></td><td></td><td></td><td></td><td></td><td></td></tr>
<tr><td></td><td></td><td></td><td></td><td></td><td></td><td></td><td></td><td></td><td></td></tr>
<tr><td></td><td></td><td></td><td></td><td></td><td></td><td></td><td></td><td></td><td></td></tr>
<tr><td></td><td></td><td></td><td></td><td></td><td></td><td></td><td></td><td></td><td></td></tr>
<tr><td></td><td></td><td></td><td></td><td></td><td></td><td></td><td></td><td></td><td></td></tr>
<tr><td></td><td></td><td></td><td></td><td></td><td></td><td></td><td></td><td></td><td></td></tr>
</table>

35.5 Adding Suffixes

Add the suffix to each word.

1. *run + er* _____

2. *plan + ing* _____

3. *sun + y* _____

4. *thin + er* _____

5. *step + ed* _____

6. *scrub + er* _____

7. *trap + ed* _____

8. *sob + ing* _____

9. *sled + ing* _____

10. *fun + y* _____

35.6 Accent

Read the words aloud. Mark the accented syllable in each word.

o pen	be gin
for get	cous in
buck et	bul le tin
con trol	pref er ence
ca ter	to mor row
com mit	sud den ly

35.7 Adding Suffixes

Add the suffix to each word.

1. open + er = _____
2. commit + ing = _____
3. commit + ee = _____
4. control + ed = _____
5. control + s = _____
6. begin + er = _____
7. begin + ing = _____
8. forget + ing = _____
9. forget + ful = _____
10. equip + ed = _____
11. equip + ment = _____
12. prefer + ed = _____
13. prefer + ence = _____
14. prefer + able = _____
15. medal + ist = _____

35.8 Adding Suffixes Flow Chart

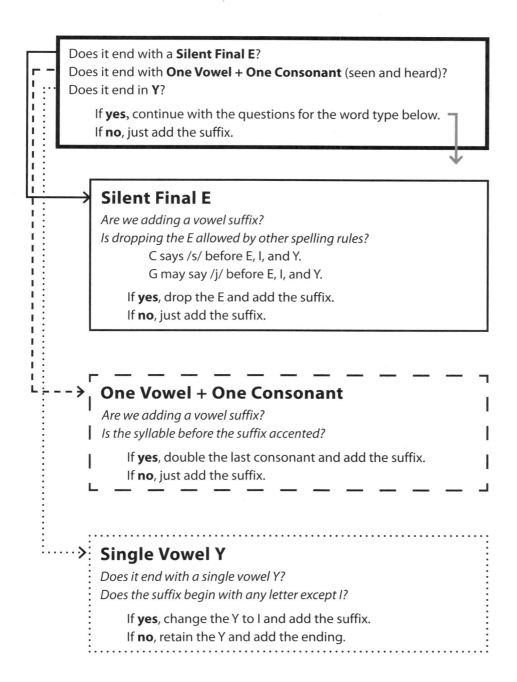

Does it end with a **Silent Final E**?
Does it end with **One Vowel + One Consonant** (seen and heard)?
Does it end in **Y**?

If **yes**, continue with the questions for the word type below.
If **no**, just add the suffix.

Silent Final E

Are we adding a vowel suffix?
Is dropping the E allowed by other spelling rules?
C says /s/ before E, I, and Y.
G may say /j/ before E, I, and Y.

If **yes**, drop the E and add the suffix.
If **no**, just add the suffix.

One Vowel + One Consonant

Are we adding a vowel suffix?
Is the syllable before the suffix accented?

If **yes**, double the last consonant and add the suffix.
If **no**, just add the suffix.

Single Vowel Y

Does it end with a single vowel Y?
Does the suffix begin with any letter except I?

If **yes**, change the Y to I and add the suffix.
If **no**, retain the Y and add the ending.

35.9 Adding a Suffix to Any Word

Write the words as your teacher reads them.

1. _____

2. _____

3. _____

4. _____

5. _____

6. _____

7. _____

8. _____

9. _____

10. _____

11. _____

12. _____

13. _____

14. _____

15. _____

16. _____

Extra Practice

35.10 Contractions

Write the contractions.

1. *I + will =* _____

2. *I + have =* _____

3. *you + will =* _____

4. *I + would =* _____

5. *he + would =* _____

6. *they + would =* _____

7. *we + would =* _____

8. *you + have =* _____

9. *she + will =* _____

10. *it + will =* _____

11. *they + have =* _____

12. *we + will =* _____

13. *they + will =* _____

14. *you + would =* _____

15. *we + have =* _____

35.11 Phonogram Practice

Write the phonograms as your teacher dictates them.

1. _____	19. _____	37. _____	55. _____
2. _____	20. _____	38. _____	56. _____
3. _____	21. _____	39. _____	57. _____
4. _____	22. _____	40. _____	58. _____
5. _____	23. _____	41. _____	59. _____
6. _____	24. _____	42. _____	60. _____
7. _____	25. _____	43. _____	61. _____
8. _____	26. _____	44. _____	62. _____
9. _____	27. _____	45. _____	63. _____
10. _____	28. _____	46. _____	64. _____
11. _____	29. _____	47. _____	65. _____
12. _____	30. _____	48. _____	66. _____
13. _____	31. _____	49. _____	67. _____
14. _____	32. _____	50. _____	68. _____
15. _____	33. _____	51. _____	69. _____
16. _____	34. _____	52. _____	70. _____
17. _____	35. _____	53. _____	
18. _____	36. _____	54. _____	

Extra Practice

35.12 Phonogram Tic-Tac-Toe

Write in the phonograms which need practice randomly on the boards. Play Phonogram Tic-Tac-Toe.

Lesson 36

36.1 Phonogram Practice

Write the phonograms as your teacher dictates them.

1. _____
2. _____
3. _____
4. _____
5. _____

6. _____
7. _____
8. _____
9. _____
10. _____

11. _____
12. _____
13. _____
14. _____
15. _____

16. _____
17. _____
18. _____
19. _____
20. _____

36.2 I Says Long /ē/

Read the words. Underline the suffix that was added.

fuzziest   curlier   juicier   pickier

36.3 Foreign Words Ending in I

Read the words. Underline I saying /ē/.

ravioli   broccoli   safari   salami

chili   ski   taxi   spaghetti

36.4 I Says Long /ē/

Read the words. Slashes been added to each word to divide the syllables.

me/di /um   sta/di/um   mil/len/ni/um

he /li /um   am/phib/i/an   his/tor/i/an

ra/di/o   bac/ter/i/a   im/me/di/ate/ly

pat/i/o   ab/bre/vi/a/tion

stud/i/o   mem/or/i/al

LIST 36

Spelling Words	Part of Speech	Plural Past Tense
1.		
2.		
3.		
4.		
5.		
6.		
7.		
8.		
9.		
10.		
11.		
12.		
13.		
14.		
15.		

36.5 Question Words

Write the question words below.

1. _____   5. _____

2. _____   6. _____

3. _____   7. _____

4. _____   8. _____

36.6 Identifying Parts of Speech

Label the parts of speech in your workbook as I write them on the board.

People will believe you.

We went on a lovely vacation with their family to the beach.

Eva will receive an award for her performance.

36.7 Who? or Whom?

Fill in the blank with the correct form of "who" or "whom."

1. _____ *asked the question?*

2. _____ *did you invite to the*
party?

3. *Before* _____ *did you speak?*

4. *About* _____ *was the book?*

5. _____ *stole the radio?*

6. _____ *believes this is the correct*
answer?

7. *To* _____ *it may concern,*

36.8 Composition

Write two questions about each statement.

310 million people live in the United States.

1. _____

2. _____

We are learning about pronouns in class today.

1. _____

2. _____

The students asked the teacher many questions after class.

1. _____

2. _____

36.9 Contractions with Not

Read the contractions aloud.

weren't	can't	won't
hasn't	wouldn't	didn't
haven't	doesn't	
wasn't	don't	
isn't	shouldn't	
couldn't	aren't	

36.10 Contractions

Write the contractions.

1. *that + is* = _____
2. *you + will* = _____
3. *are + not* = _____
4. *will + not* = _____
5. *they + are* = _____
6. *have + not* = _____
7. *should + not* = _____
8. *there + is* = _____
9. *I + would* = _____
10. *she + will* = _____

36.11 Dictation

Listen to each sentence as your teacher reads it aloud. Repeat it back. Write it on the lines below.

1. _____

_____

2. _____

_____

3. _____

_____

4. _____

_____

5. _____

_____

6. _____

_____

Lesson 37

37

37.1 The Advanced Phonogram OUR

Read the words. Underline the OUR.

adjourn	flourish	nourish
courtesy	journal	sojourner
courage	journey	tournament

37.2 American and British Spelling

Read the American and British spellings of each word. Underline the phonogram used to spell the sound /er/.

American Spelling	British Spelling
color	colour
behavior	behaviour
labor	labour
neighbor	neighbour
honor	honour
valor	valour
enamor	enamour
favor	favour
flavor	flavour
glamor	glamour

37.3 Writing the Phonogram

Write the new phonogram five times and say it aloud.

our _____

_____

37.4 Phonogram Practice

Write the phonograms as your teacher dictates them.

1. _____	6. _____	11. _____	16. _____
2. _____	7. _____	12. _____	17. _____
3. _____	8. _____	13. _____	18. _____
4. _____	9. _____	14. _____	19. _____
5. _____	10. _____	15. _____	20. _____

37.5 Distorted U

Read each word slowly and clearly pronouncing each sound. Then blend it together more quickly. Underline the part of the word with a distorted sound.

closure	sugar	moisture	feature
measure	sure	adventure	creature
treasure	picture	mixture	texture
pleasure	nature	culture	

LIST 37

Spelling Words	Part of Speech	Plural Past Tense
1.		
2.		
3.		
4.		
5.		
6.		
7.		
8.		
9.		
10.		
11.		
12.		
13.		
14.		
15.		

37.6 Coordinating Conjunctions

Write the seven coordinating conjunctions as your teacher dictates them.

1. _____

2. _____

3. _____

4. _____

5. _____

6. _____

7. _____

37.7 Junctions

37.8 Coordinating Conjunctions

Read the sentences. Circle the comma, underline the coordinating conjunction.

1. Tom was not in class today, nor will he be here tomorrow.

2. Evan received three letters from the school, but I did not receive any.

3. She must finish her homework before six o'clock, or she will have to miss the movie.

4. My younger sister loves to travel, yet she did not want to go on this trip.

5. Eli was late, so we started without him.

37.9 Joining Sentences

Join the sentences using a comma and coordinating conjunction.

Joy took my picture again. She did not take my brother's picture even once.

1. _____

_____

_____

Mother has encouraged her in every way possible. She still wants to quit.

2. _____

_____

_____

I am not sure how to do this problem. I do not know how to start.

3. _____

_____

_____

The exam was very easy. We finished early.

4. _____

_____

_____

The class must memorize all the words before the test tomorrow. They will not go on to the next chapter.

5. _____

_____

_____

37.10 Grammar Rule

Follow the directions given by your teacher.

_____

Definition

_____

_____

_____

37.11 To, Too, or Two

Complete each sentence with to, too, or two.

1. Do not open the door _____ wide.

2. The children will walk _____ school.

3. You need to memorize _____ verses of the poem.

4. The teachers are going _____ a workshop.

5. We have _____ much fruit.

6. I would wear a coat _____ .

7. Please put _____ scoops of sugar in the pitcher.

37.12 Dictation

Listen to each sentence as your teacher reads it aloud. Repeat it back. Write it on the lines below.

1. _____

_____

_____

2. _____

_____

_____

3. _____

_____

_____

4. _____

_____

_____

5. _____

_____

_____

6. _____

_____

37.13 Composition

Write three sentences using a coordinating conjunction.

and   for

or   nor

yet   but

so

1. _____

_____

_____

2. _____

_____

_____

3. _____

_____

_____

37.14 Vocabulary

Add the prefix. Discuss the meaning of each word.

en + close = _____

en + act = _____

en + gulf = _____

en + danger = _____

en + liven = _____

dis + agree = _____

dis + courage = _____

dis + cover = _____

dis + appoint = _____

dis + connect = _____

Lesson 38

38.1 AIGH

Follow your teacher's instructions.

_____

38.2 Writing

Write straight five times.

straight

_____

_____

_____

38.3 Phonogram Practice

Write the phonograms as your teacher dictates them.

1. _____   6. _____   11. _____   16. _____

2. _____   7. _____   12. _____   17. _____

3. _____   8. _____   13. _____   18. _____

4. _____   9. _____   14. _____   19. _____

5. _____   10. _____   15. _____   20. _____

38.4 I says /y/

Read the words. When does I say /y/?

onion	billion	genius
union	stallion	valiant
opinion	savior	
million	senior	

LIST 38

Spelling Words	Part of Speech	Plural Past Tense
1.		
2.		
3.		
4.		
5.		
6.		
7.		
8.		
9.		
10.		
11.		
12.		
13.		
14.		
15.		

38.5 Sentences and Fragments

Read the sentences and phrases. If it is a complete sentence, put an S before it. If it is fragment, put a F before it. If it a fragment, underline the word that is stealing the completeness of the sentences.

1. _____S_____   I memorized my math facts.

2. _____F_____   <u>When</u> I memorized my math facts.

3. _____   He rode in an airplane.

4. _____   Although he rode in an airplane.

5. _____   I want to surprise my friend.

6. _____   Unless I want to surprise my friend.

7. _____   Evan and Sam hiked up the mountain together.

8. _____   Because Evan and Sam hiked up the mountain together.

9. _____   Finish your science.

10. _____   If you finish your science.

11. _____   I walk the dog.

12. _____   Whenever I walk the dog.

13. _____   Molly went to the store.

14. _____   Since Molly went to the store.

38.6 List of Subordinating Conjunctions

Read the subordinating conjunctions aloud. Practice using them in sentences aloud.

after	if	supposing
although	in case	the first time
as	in order that	than
as if	in the event that	though
as long as	inasmuch	unless
as much as	just in case	until
as soon as	lest	when
as though	now that	whenever
because	once	where
before	only if	whereas
by the time	provided that	wherever
even if	rather than	whether or not
even though	since	while
every time	so that	

38.7 Sentences

Combine the sentences using the subordinating conjunction.

1. (Although) That is a good combination. I do not want to try it.

_____

_____

2. (While) I waited for the eye doctor. I read a book.

_____

_____

3. You may miss the announcement. (unless) You listen to the radio this afternoon.

_____

_____

4. (When) Spain plays Brazil. I will cheer for Spain.

_____

_____

5. That sweater is too small for him. (because) It is a size medium.

_____

_____

38.8 Grammar Rule

Follow the directions given by your teacher.

_____

Definition

_____

_____

_____

Write seven examples of subordinating conjunctions.

1. _____   5. _____

2. _____   6. _____

3. _____   7. _____

4. _____

38.9 Identifying Parts of Speech

Mark the parts of speech while your teacher marks them on the board.

While Father went to the store for more milk, I made dinner.

We must leave immediately because class starts in three minutes.

I listen to the radio until I leave for school.

38.10 Dictation

Listen to each sentence as your teacher reads it aloud. Repeat it back. Write it on the lines below.

1. _____

_____

_____

2. _____

_____

_____

3. _____

_____

_____

4. _____

_____

_____

5. _____

_____

_____

6. _____

_____

38.11 Composition

Write two sentences beginning with a subordinating conjunction. Then rewrite each sentence with the subordinating conjunction in the middle of the sentence.

although	whenever	if
since	because	after
when	unless	before

1. _____

_____

_____

_____

_____

_____

2. _____

_____

_____

_____

_____

38.12 Compound Words

Combine each of the words with *eye* to form new compound words.

ball	brow	witness
lash	glasses	sight

1. _____

2. _____

3. _____

4. _____

5. _____

6. _____

Combine each of the words with *straight* to form new compound words.

forward	laced	jacket
edge	away	

1. _____

2. _____

3. _____

4. _____

5. _____

Lesson 39

39.1 The Advanced Phonogram SC

Read the words. Underline the SC.

1. scene
2. science
3. scent
4. scepter

5. discipline
6. fascinate
7. scissors
8. ascent

9. descend
10. discern

39.2 Writing the Phonogram

Write the new phonogram five times and say it aloud.

sc

39.3 Phonogram Practice

Write the phonograms as your teacher dictates them.

1. _____   6. _____   11. _____   16. _____

2. _____   7. _____   12. _____   17. _____

3. _____   8. _____   13. _____   18. _____

4. _____   9. _____   14. _____   19. _____

5. _____   10. _____   15. _____   20. _____

LIST 39

Spelling Words	Part of Speech	Plural Past Tense
1.		
2.		
3.		
4.		
5.		
6.		
7.		
8.		
9.		
10.		
11.		
12.		
13.		
14.		
15.		

39.4 Subordinating Conjunctions

Write the subordinating conjunctions as your teacher dictates them.

1. _____

2. _____

3. _____

4. _____

5. _____

6. _____

7. _____

8. _____

9. _____

10. _____

11. _____

12. _____

13. _____

14. _____

39.5 Sentences

Underline the two clauses. Highlight the subordinating conjunction. (Hint: the subordinating conjunctions all have two words or more.)

1. As long as the stadium is empty, we can sit together.

2. Even if you stop the motor, it will not make a difference.

3. I will not spend another dollar even though you say it is a good deal.

4. She marched into the store as though she owned it.

5. In the event that Dad arrives home in the next hour, we will leave on vacation today.

6. Bring an umbrella with you in case it begins to rain.

7. By the time the earth has orbited around the sun one time, the moon has orbited around the earth more than thirteen times.

39.6 Identifying Parts of Speech

Write the parts of speech for each sentence as your teacher writes them on the board.

1. Even though I studied hard for the science test, I received a poor grade.

2. As long as they are constructing the new stadium, we cannot drive

    down this street.

3. Even though he has saved fifty-five dollars, it is not enough.

39.7 Composition

Write two sentences beginning with a subordinating conjunction. Then rewrite each sentence with the subordinating conjunction in the middle of the sentence.

1. _____

_____

_____

_____

_____

_____

2. _____

_____

_____

_____

_____

_____

39.8 Latin Roots

Read the words. What is similar between each of the words?

motor	locomotive	immovable
motion	emotion	mobile
motionless	motel	mobility
motive	movie	automobile
motivate	move	bookmobile
motivation	movable	immobile
motorist	movement	immobilize
promote	remove	snowmobile
demote	removal	
remote	unmovable	

39.9 Synonyms

Which words in *39.8 Latin Roots* share the same meaning?

_____

_____

_____

_____

_____

_____

_____

39.10 Dictation

Listen to each sentence as your teacher reads it aloud. Repeat it back. Write it on the lines below.

1. _____

_____

_____

2. _____

_____

_____

3. _____

_____

_____

4. _____

_____

_____

5. _____

_____

_____

6. _____

_____

Lesson 40

40

40.1 Assessment

Listen to each phrase as your teacher dictates. Repeat it back. Write it on the lines below.

1. _____

   _____

2. _____

   _____

3. _____

   _____

4. _____

   _____

5. _____

   _____

6. _____

   _____

7. _____

   _____

8. _____

_____

9. _____

_____

10. _____

_____

40.2 Reading

Read the sentences.

1. Nine million people live in the country of Sweden.

2. A century is one hundred years.

3. When you see them together, will you take a picture for me?

4. The earth is beautiful.

5. After the construction is finished, we will have more room.

6. Which section do I need to practice again?

7. Our team will play against Century High School.

8. She will not be happy until she has another pet.

9. Before you leave, I'd like to ask you something.

10. This shirt is a medium.

11. Why won't this motor work?

12. I learned the new motions easily because they are so easy.

13. She is good at memorization.

14. While it was an unusual situation, they still should have responded immediately.

15. Where was the accident?

16. The calendar is in the kitchen.

40.3 Words to Practice

Mark the spelling words which need more practice.

1. _____ about	22. _____ equipment	43. _____ straight
2. _____ after	23. _____ eye	44. _____ sugar
3. _____ again	24. _____ happen	45. _____ sure
4. _____ against	25. _____ how	46. _____ sweet
5. _____ also	26. _____ immediately	47. _____ together
6. _____ although	27. _____ impossible	48. _____ too
7. _____ another	28. _____ measure	49. _____ unless
8. _____ because	29. _____ medium	50. _____ until
9. _____ before	30. _____ memorization	51. _____ unusual
10. _____ believe	31. _____ memorize	52. _____ what
11. _____ calendar	32. _____ million	53. _____ when
12. _____ century	33. _____ motion	54. _____ whenever
13. _____ combination	34. _____ motive	55. _____ where
14. _____ construction	35. _____ motor	56. _____ which
15. _____ country	36. _____ picture	57. _____ while
16. _____ difference	37. _____ problem	58. _____ who
17. _____ dollar	38. _____ question	59. _____ whose
18. _____ earth	39. _____ radio	60. _____ why
19. _____ easy	40. _____ science	
20. _____ encouraging	41. _____ since	
21. _____ enough	42. _____ stadium	

40.4 Adding Suffixes to One-Syllable Words

Add the suffix to each word.

1. add + ed

2. fog + y

3. dad + y

4. sweat + er

5. bat + er

6. sad + ly

7. quit + er

8. pack + ing

9. run + er

10. slip + ed

40.5 Adding Suffixes to Multi-Syllable Words

Add the suffix to each word.

1. control + er _____

2. forget + ing _____

3. commit + ee _____

4. cancel + ation _____

5. medal + ist _____

6. begin + er _____

7. omit + ed _____

8. prefer + ed _____

9. rebel + ion _____

10. equip + ing _____

11. open + er _____

40.6 Coordinating Conjunctions

Join the sentences using a comma and a coordinating conjunction.

This medium size shirt is too small. (but) The large one fits well.

1. _____

_____

_____

It is not a problem for me. (for) I have plenty of time to work on it.

2. _____

_____

_____

We need to stick together at the concert. (so) No one gets separated from our group.

3. _____

_____

_____

I added too much sugar to the lemonade. (and) Now she doesn't want to drink it.

4. _____

_____

_____

40.7 Sentences and Fragments

Write a S next to the complete sentences. Write an F next to the fragments. Underline the word(s) that turn the sentence into a fragment.

1. _____*F*_____   <u>While</u> I solved the problem.

2. _____   The students asked many questions.

3. _____   Whenever I listen to the radio.

4. _____   The stadium is full of cheering fans.

5. _____   My teacher encouraged me to learn to play guitar.

6. _____   As soon as the construction is finished.

7. _____   If we have enough equipment.

8. _____   The sugar is in the top cupboard.

40.8 Subordinating Conjunctions

Reverse the order of the two clauses. Rewrite the sentence.

We swam a lot this summer because it has been unusually hot.

1. _____

_____

_____

The first time I took a picture with that camera, it did not turn out well.

2. _____

_____

_____

Even though my coach believed in me, I didn't feel encouraged.

3. _____

_____

_____

I will give you twenty-five dollars if you help me move this equipment.

4. _____

_____

_____

40.9 Phonogram Practice

Write the phonograms as your teacher dictates them.

1. _____	20. _____	39. _____	58. _____
2. _____	21. _____	40. _____	59. _____
3. _____	22. _____	41. _____	60. _____
4. _____	23. _____	42. _____	61. _____
5. _____	24. _____	43. _____	62. _____
6. _____	25. _____	44. _____	63. _____
7. _____	26. _____	45. _____	64. _____
8. _____	27. _____	46. _____	65. _____
9. _____	28. _____	47. _____	66. _____
10. _____	29. _____	48. _____	67. _____
11. _____	30. _____	49. _____	68. _____
12. _____	31. _____	50. _____	69. _____
13. _____	32. _____	51. _____	70. _____
14. _____	33. _____	52. _____	71. _____
15. _____	34. _____	53. _____	72. _____
16. _____	35. _____	54. _____	73. _____
17. _____	36. _____	55. _____	74. _____
18. _____	37. _____	56. _____	
19. _____	38. _____	57. _____	